Charles Woodruff Shields

A manual of worship, suitable to be used in national and state legislatures

Charles Woodruff Shields

A manual of worship, suitable to be used in national and state legislatures

ISBN/EAN: 9783337284046

Printed in Europe, USA, Canada, Australia, Japan

Cover: Foto ©Suzi / pixelio.de

More available books at **www.hansebooks.com**

A

MANUAL OF WORSHIP,

SUITABLE TO BE USED

IN LEGISLATIVE AND OTHER PUBLIC BODIES,
IN THE ARMY AND NAVY,
AND IN MILITARY AND NAVAL ACADEMIES, ASYLUMS,
HOSPITALS, ETC.

Compiled

FROM THE FORMS AND IN ACCORDANCE WITH THE COMMON USAGES
OF ALL CHRISTIAN DENOMINATIONS.

And jointly recommended

BY EMINENT CLERGYMEN OF VARIOUS PERSUASIONS.

PHILADELPHIA:
GEORGE W. CHILDS,
628 AND 630 CHESTNUT STREET.
1862.

The compiler of this Manual, having submitted it to the examination of eminent clergymen in different denominations, has permission to append their names to the joint recommendation on the ensuing page.

CHARLES W. SHIELDS.

PHILADELPHIA, *Nov.* 1862.

RECOMMENDATION.

The undersigned cordially unite in recommending this MANUAL OF WORSHIP as suitable for discretionary use in National and State Legislatures, in the Army and Navy, and in Military and Naval Institutions, in cases where our own respective rules and customs of worship cannot be exclusively maintained.

REV. ALBERT BARNES, Pastor of the First Presbyterian Church, (N. S.,) Philadelphia.

REV. H. W. BELLOWS, D. D., Minister to the First Congregational Church, (Unitarian,) New York.

REV. H. A. BOARDMAN, Pastor of the Tenth Presbyterian Church, (O. S.,) Philadelphia.

REV. CHARLES D. COOPER, D. D., Rector of St. Philip's Church, Philadelphia.

REV. J. B. DALES, D. D., Pastor of the First United Presbyterian Church, Philadelphia.

REV. THOMAS DE WITT, D. D., Pastor of Collegiate Reformed Dutch Church, New York.

REV. J. P. DURBIN, D. D , Methodist Episcopal Church, New York.

REV. H. HARBAUGH, D. D., Pastor of St. John's Church, (German Reformed), Lebanon, Pa.

REV. CHARLES HODGE, D.D., Professor of Theology, Princeton, N.J.

REV. C. P. KRAUTH, D. D., Evangelical Lutheran Church, Philadelphia.

RIGHT REV. C. P. McILVAINE, D.D., D.C.L., Protestant Episcopal Church, Diocese of Ohio.

RIGHT REV. ALONZO POTTER, D.D., LL.D., Protestant Episcopal Church, Diocese of Pennsylvania.

REV. BARNAS SEARS, D.D., President of Brown University, Providence, R. I.

REV. THOMAS H. STOCKTON. D.D., Methodist Protestant Church.

REV. THATCHER THAYER, D. D., Pastor of the Congregational Church, Newport, R I.

REV. JOS. P. THOMPSON, D D., Pastor of the Tabernacle (Congregational) Church, New York.

REV. WILLIAM R. WILLIAMS, D.D., Pastor of the Baptist Church on Amity Street, New York.

REV. THEODORE D. WOOLSEY, D. D., LL.D., President of Yale College, New Haven, Conn.

CONTENTS.

1*

NOTE.

THE Forms of Worship in this Manual are derived from the Holy Scriptures and the ancient Christian liturgies, except a few selections from various modern formularies, and some needed examples not afforded by such sources. They contain nothing sectarian or denominational; and are here arranged upon the principle of retaining as much as possible of what is common to all Christian people, and as little as possible of what is peculiar to any.

In the absence of clergymen, the Manual may be used by laymen.

The Service may be varied and adapted to particular occasions and circumstances by the use of other examples than those given in each Form; and to aid in selecting for this purpose, complete Tables of Scripture Lessons, Psalms, Hymns and Prayers are given at the end of the Manual.

Any particular parts or expressions which do not commend themselves can easily be omitted.

A FORM OF DIVINE SERVICE

SUITABLE TO BE USED IN THE

ARMY AND NAVY, AND IN MILITARY AND NAVAL ACADEMIES, ASYLUMS, HOSPITALS, ETC.

Divine Service may begin with the reading of the following words of Holy Scripture:

THUS saith the High and Lofty One that inhabiteth eternity, whose name is Holy: I dwell in the high and holy place, with him also that is of a contrite and humble spirit, to revive the spirit of the humble and to revive the heart of the contrite ones. For I will not contend forever, neither will I be always angry.

And if we say that we have no sin, we deceive ourselves and the truth is not in us; but if we confess our sins he is faithful and just to forgive us our sins, and to cleanse us from all unrighteousness.

Let us therefore come boldly unto the

throne of grace, that we may obtain mercy
and find grace to help in time of need :—

And then prayer may be offered, consisting of the *Confession* and *Invocation*, which here follow, and concluding
with the *Lord's Prayer*.

A General Confession.

ALMIGHTY God, our Righteous Judge
and King Eternal, we confess to
Thee, that in many times and ways, by
thought, word, and deed, we have exceedingly sinned against Thee; and through
our fault; through our fault alone; through
our most grievous fault, provoked thy
wrath and punishment. But we humbly
beseech Thee, O holy and loving Father,
of thy great mercy to forgive us our offences, and henceforth grant us true re-
pentance and newness of life, for the
honor of thy holy Name.

An Invocation.

HEAR us, O Holy Father, Almighty
Lord, Everlasting God! and vouchsafe to pour down thy Holy Spirit on all
that are here assembled; that, being
cleansed and illumined by his grace, we
may worthily celebrate thy praise, meekly

learn thy word, render due thanks for thy mercies, and obtain a gracious answer to our prayers, through the merits of Jesus Christ our Lord.

The Lord's Prayer.

OUR Father, who art in heaven; Hallowed be thy name; Thy kingdom come; Thy will be done on earth, as it is in heaven; Give us this day our daily bread; And forgive us our trespasses, as we forgive those who trespass against us; And lead us not into temptation; But deliver us from evil; . For thine is the kingdom, and the power, and the glory, for ever and ever. Amen.

Then may be sung one of the *Hymns,* or the following *Psalm* or some other *Psalm,* selected from the Table of Psalms (see page 127) may be read.

Psalm lxvii.

GOD be merciful unto us, and bless us; and cause his face to shine upon us.

That thy way may be known upon earth, thy saving health among all nations.

Let the people praise thee, O God; let all the people praise thee.

O let the nations be glad and sing for

joy; for thou shalt judge the people righteously, and govern the nations upon earth.

Let the people praise thee, O God; let all the people praise thee.

Then shall the earth yield her increase; and God, even our own God, shall bless us.

God shall bless us; and all the ends of the earth shall fear him.

Then may be read a portion of the Holy Scriptures, selected from the Table of Scripture Lessons (see pages 125–131). Or the Ten Commandments may be read.

The Commandments.

GOD spake all these words, saying, I am the Lord thy God, which have brought thee out of the land of Egypt, out of the house of bondage.

I. Thou shalt have no other gods before me.

II. Thou shalt not make unto thee any graven image, or any likeness of any thing that is in heaven above, or that is in the earth beneath, or that is in the water under the earth: thou shalt not bow down thyself to them nor serve them:

for I the Lord thy God am a jealous God. visiting the iniquity of the fathers upon the children unto the third and fourth generation of them that hate me; and showing mercy unto thousands of them that love me and keep my commandments.

III. Thou shalt not take the name of the Lord thy God in vain; for the Lord will not hold him guiltless that taketh his name in vain.

IV. Remember the Sabbath-day, to keep it holy. Six days shalt thou labor, and do all thy work: but the seventh day is the Sabbath of the Lord thy God: in it thou shalt not do any work, thou, nor thy son, nor thy daughter, thy man-servant, nor thy maid-servant, nor thy cattle, nor thy stranger that is within thy gates: for in six days the Lord made heaven and earth, the sea, and all that in them is, and rested the seventh day: wherefore the Lord blessed the Sabbath-day, and hallowed it.

V. Honor thy father and thy mother;

that thy days may be long upon the land
which the Lord thy God giveth thee.

VI. Thou shalt not kill.

VII. Thou shalt not commit adultery.

VIII. Thou shalt not steal.

IX. Thou shalt not bear false witness
against thy neighbor.

X. Thou shalt not covet thy neighbor's
house, thou shalt not covet thy neighbor's
wife, nor his man-servant, nor his maid-
servant, nor his ox, nor his ass, nor any
thing that is thy neighbor's.

Our Lord Jesus Christ also saith :

Thou shalt love the Lord thy God with
all thy heart, and with all thy soul, and
with all thy mind.   This is the first and
great commandment.   And the second is
like unto it : Thou shalt love thy neighbor as thyself.   On these two commandments hang all the law and the prophets.
Think not that I am come to destroy the
law or the prophets : I am not come to
destroy but to fulfill.

And when the reading of the Scriptures is finished, the
Apostles' Creed may be recited.

W E BELIEVE in God the Father Almighty, Maker of heaven and earth:

And in Jesus Christ his only Son, our Lord; Who was conceived by the Holy Ghost, Born of the Virgin Mary; Suffered under Pontius Pilate, Was crucified, dead, and buried; He descended into hell, The third day he rose again from the dead; He ascended into heaven, And sitteth on the right hand of God the Father Almighty; From thence he shall come to judge the quick and the dead.

We believe in the Holy Ghost; The holy Catholic Church, the Communion of Saints; The forgiveness of sins; The Resurrection of the body; And the life everlasting. Amen.

Then may be offered the following *General Prayers*, or a portion of them, together with any *Special Prayers* which the occasion shall require. (See page 131.)

LET thy merciful ears, O Lord, be open to the prayers of thy humble servants; and that they may obtain their petitions, make them to ask such things

2

as shall please thee; through Jesus Christ
our Lord.

O GOD, the Father of Heaven, have
mercy upon us miserable sinners.

O God the Son, Redeemer of the World,
have mercy upon us miserable sinners.

O God the Holy Ghost, proceeding from
the Father and the Son, have mercy upon
us miserable sinners.

O holy, blessed, and glorious Trinity,
three Persons and one God, have mercy
upon us miserable sinners.

Remember not, Lord, our offences, nor
the offences of our forefathers: neither
take thou vengeance of our sins: spare us,
O Lord; spare thy people, whom thou
hast redeemed with thy most precious
blood, and be not angry with us forever.

Deliver us, O Lord,
From all evil and mischief; from sin;
from the crafts and assaults of the devil;
from thy wrath, and from everlasting dam-
nation.

Deliver us, O Lord,
From all blindness of heart; from pride,

vain-glory and hypocrisy; from envy, hatred and malice, and all uncharitableness; from inordinate affections and deadly sins, and from all the deceits of the world, the flesh, and the devil.

Deliver us, O Lord,

From lightning and tempest; from plague, pestilence and famine; from battle, and murder, and from sudden death.

Deliver us, O Lord,

From all sedition, privy conspiracy, and rebellion; from all false doctrine, heresy and schism; from hardness of heart, and contempt of thy word and commandment.

Deliver us, O Lord,

By the mystery of thy holy Incarnation; by thy Baptism, Fasting, and Temptation; by thine Agony and Bloody Sweat; by thy Cross and Passion; by thy precious Death and Burial; by thy glorious Resurrection and Ascension; and by the coming of the Holy Ghost.

Deliver us, O Lord,

In all time of our tribulation; in all time of our prosperity; in the hour of death, and in the day of judgment.

A General Intercession.

WE sinners do beseech thee, O Lord God,
That it may please thee to rule and govern thy holy church universal in the right way; to preserve all Christian ministers and people in soundness of word and holiness of life; to put an end to all sects and scandals; and to send forth faithful laborers into thy harvest.

We beseech thee, O Lord God,
That it may please thee to plenteously endue with heavenly wisdom and grace thy servants, the *President*, the *Judges*, and the *Congress* of the *United States*, and all others in authority; to strengthen and defend our Army and Navy, giving them the victory over all thine and our enemies; to maintain truth and righteousness among the people; and to give to our land the blessings of peace and freedom; of knowledge, virtue and piety.

We beseech thee, O Lord God,
That it may please thee to cleanse the world from all errors; to take away diseases; to keep off famine; open prisons:

loosen chains; bind up the broken-hearted;
bring back wanderers; give health to the
sick; and to mariners a port of safety.

We beseech thee, O Lord God,
That it may please thee to give to all nations unity, peace, and concord; to govern
and guide all rulers and peoples in ways
of justice and truth; and to hasten the
promised time of peace.

Here may be offered any *Special Prayers* which the
occasion requires.

A General Thanksgiving.

ALMIGHTY God, Father of all mercies, we thine unworthy servants,
do give thee most humble and hearty
thanks for all thy goodness and loving-
kindness to us, and to all men. We bless
thee for our creation, preservation, and
all the blessings of this life; but above all,
for thine inestimable love in the redemp-
tion of the world by our Lord Jesus Christ;
for the means of grace, and for the hope
of glory. And we beseech thee, give us
that due sense of all thy mercies, that our
hearts may be unfeignedly thankful, and
that we may show forth thy praise, not

2*

only with our lips, but in our lives; by giving up ourselves to thy service, and by walking before thee in holiness and right-eousness all our days; through Jesus Christ our Lord, to whom, with thee and the Holy Ghost, be all honor and glory, world without end.

A Concluding Prayer.

ALMIGHTY God, who hast given us grace at this time with one accord to make our common supplications unto thee; and dost promise that when two or three are gathered together in thy name thou wilt grant their requests; fulfil now, O Lord, the desires and petitions of thy servants, as may be most expedient for them; granting us in this world knowledge of thy truth, and in the world to come life everlasting. Amen.

And then may be sung a *Hymn*, or the following *Hymn* may be read.

A General Hymn of Praise.

WE praise thee, O God; we acknow-ledge thee to be the Lord.

All the earth doth worship thee, the Father everlasting.

To thee all angels cry aloud; the heavens and all the powers therein.

To thee Cherubim and Seraphim continually do cry,

Holy, holy, holy, Lord God of Sabaoth!

Heaven and earth are full of the majesty of thy glory.

The glorious company of the apostles praise thee.

The goodly fellowship of the prophets praise thee.

The noble army of the martyrs praise thee.

The holy Church throughout the world doth acknowledge thee,

The Father of an infinite majesty;

Thine adorable, true, and only Son;

Also the Holy Ghost, the Comforter.

Thou art the King of glory, O Christ.

Thou art the everlasting Son of the Father.

When thou tookest upon thee to deliver man, thou didst humble thyself to be born of a virgin.

When thou hadst overcome the sharpness of death, thou didst open the kingdom of heaven to all believers.

Thou sittest at the right hand of God, in the glory of the Father.

We believe that thou shalt come to be our Judge.

We therefore pray thee, help thy servants, whom thou hast redeemed with thy precious blood.

Make them to be numbered with thy saints, in glory everlasting.

O Lord, save thy people, and bless thine heritage.

Govern them and lift them up forever.

Day by day we magnify thee;

And we worship thy name ever, world without end.

Vouchsafe, O Lord, to keep us this day without sin.

O Lord, have mercy on us, have mercy on us.

O Lord, let thy mercy be upon us, as our trust is in thee.

O Lord, in thee have we trusted; let us never be confounded. Amen.

And then the *Collection* may be taken, if any have been appointed. And also religious notices may be given.

Then may follow the *Sermon;* or, in the absence of a clergyman, the following or some other one of our *Lord's Discourses* (see p. 127) may be read, or a portion may be read.

The Sermon on the Mount.

AND seeing the multitudes, he went up into a mountain: and when he was set, his disciples came unto him:

And he opened his mouth, and taught them, saying,

Blessed are the poor in spirit: for theirs is the kingdom of heaven.

Blessed are they that mourn: for they shall be comforted.

Blessed are the meek; for they shall inherit the earth.

Blessed are they which do hunger and thirst after righteousness: for they shall be filled.

Blessed are the merciful: for they shall obtain mercy.

Blessed are the pure in heart; for they shall see God.

Blessed are the peacemakers: for they shall be called the children of God.

Blessed are they which are persecuted for righteousness' sake: for theirs is the kingdom of heaven.

Blessed are ye, when men shall revile you, and persecute you, and shall say all manner of evil against you falsely, for my sake.

Rejoice, and be exceeding glad : for great is your reward in heaven : for so persecuted they the prophets which were before you.

Ye are the salt of the earth : but if the salt have lost his savour, wherewith shall it be salted? it is thenceforth good for nothing, but to be cast out, and to be trodden under foot of men.

Ye are the light of the world. A city that is set on a hill cannot be hid.

Neither do men light a candle, and put it under a bushel, but on a candlestick ; and it giveth light unto all that are in the house.

Let your light so shine before men, that they may see your good works, and glorify your father which is in heaven.

Think not that I am come to destroy the law, or the prophets : I am not come to destroy, but to fulfil.

For verily I say unto you, Till heaven and earth pass, one jot or one title shall in no wise pass from the law. till all be fulfilled.

Whosoever therefore shall break one of these least commandments, and shall teach men so, he shall be called the least in the kingdom of heaven: but whosoever shall do and teach them, the same shall be called great in the kingdom of heaven.

For I say unto you, That except your righteousness shall exceed the righteousness of the Scribes and Pharisees, ye shall in no case enter into the kingdom of heaven.

Ye have heard that it was said by them of old time, Thou shalt not kill; and whosoever shall kill shall be in danger of the judgment:

But I say unto you, That whosoever is angry with his brother without a cause shall be in danger of the judgment: and whosoever shall say to his brother, Raca, shall be in danger of the council; but whosoever shall say, Thou fool, shall be in danger of hell fire.

Therefore if thou bring thy gift to the altar, and there rememberest that thy brother hath aught against thee;

Leave there thy gift before the altar,

and go thy way; first be reconciled to thy brother, and then come and offer thy gift.

Agree with thine adversary quickly, while thou art in the way with him; lest at any time the adversary deliver thee to the judge, and the judge deliver thee to the officer, and thou be cast into prison.

Verily I say unto thee, Thou shalt by no means come out thence, till thou hast paid the uttermost farthing.

Ye have heard that it was said by them of old time, Thou shalt not commit adultery:

But I say unto you, That whosoever looketh on a woman to lust after her hath committed adultery with her already in his heart.

And if thy right eye offend thee, pluck it out, and cast it from thee: for it is profitable for thee that one of thy members should perish, and not that thy whole body should be cast into hell.

And if thy right hand offend thee, cut it off, and cast it from thee; for it is profitable for thee that one of thy members should perish, and not that thy whole body should be cast into hell.

It hath been said, Whosoever shall put away his wife, let him give her a writing of divorcement;

But I say unto you, That whosoever shall put away his wife, saving for the cause of fornication, causeth her to commit adultery : and whosoever shall marry her that is divorced committeth adultery.

Again, ye have heard that it hath been said by them of old time, Thou shalt not forswear thyself, but shall perform unto the Lord thine oaths :

But I say unto you, Swear not at all; neither by heaven; for it is God's throne:

Nor by the earth ; for it is his footstool: neither by Jerusalem; for it is the city of the great King.

Neither shalt thou swear by thy head, because thou canst not make one hair white or black.

But let your communication be, Yea, yea; Nay, nay : for whatsoever is more than these cometh of evil.

Ye have heard that it hath been said, An eye for an eye, and a tooth for a tooth.

But I say unto you, That ye resist not

3

evil; but whosoever shall smite thee on thy right cheek, turn to him the other also.

And if any man will sue thee at the law, and take away thy coat, let him have thy cloak also.

And whosoever shall compel thee to go a mile, go with him twain.

Give to him that asketh thee, and from him that would borrow of thee turn not thou away.

Ye have heard that it hath been said, Thou shalt love thy neighbor, and hate thine enemy.

But I say unto you, Love your enemies, bless them that curse you, do good to them that hate you, and pray for them which despitefully use you, and persecute you.

That ye may be the children of your Father which is in heaven; for he maketh his sun to rise on the evil and on the good, and sendeth rain on the just and on the unjust.

For if ye love them which love you, what reward have ye? do not even the publicans the same?

And if ye salute your brethren only, what do ye more than others? do not even the publicans so?

Be ye therefore perfect, even as your Father which is in heaven is perfect.

TAKE heed that ye do not your alms before men, to be seen of them: otherwise ye have no reward of your Father which is in heaven.

Therefore when thou doest thine alms, do not sound a trumpet before thee, as the hypocrites do in the synagogues and in the streets, that they may have glory of men. Verily I say unto you, They have their reward.

But when thou doest alms, let not thy left hand know what thy right hand doeth:

That thine alms may be in secret: and thy Father which seeth in secret himself shall reward thee openly.

And when thou prayest, thou shalt not be as the hypocrites are; for they love to pray standing in the synagogues and in the corners of the streets, that they may be seen of men. Verily I say unto you, They have their reward.

But thou, when thou prayest, enter into thy closet, and when thou hast shut thy door, pray to thy Father which is in secret; and thy Father which seeth in secret shall reward thee openly.

But when ye pray, use not vain repetitions, as the heathen do: for they think that they shall be heard for their much speaking.

Be not ye therefore like unto them: for your Father knoweth what things ye have need of, before ye ask him.

After this manner therefore pray ye: Our Father which art in heaven, Hallowed be thy name.

Thy kingdom come. Thy will be done in earth, as it is in heaven.

Give us this day our daily bread.

And forgive us our debts, as we forgive our debtors.

And lead us not into temptation, but deliver us from evil: For thine is the kingdom, and the power, and the glory, for ever. Amen.

For if ye forgive men their trespasses, your heavenly Father will also forgive you:

But if ye forgive not men their trespasses, neither will your Father forgive your trespasses.

Moreover when ye fast, be not, as the hypocrites, of a sad countenance : for they disfigure their faces, that they may appear unto men to fast. Verily I say unto you, They have their reward.

But thou, when thou fastest, anoint thine head, and wash thy face;

That thou appear not unto men to fast, but unto thy Father which is in secret : and thy Father which seeth in secret shall reward thee openly.

Lay not up for yourselves treasures upon earth, where moth and rust doth corrupt, and where thieves break through and steal :

But lay up for yourselves treasures in heaven, where neither moth nor rust doth corrupt, and where thieves do not break through nor steal :

For where your treasure is, there will your heart be also.

The light of the body is the eye : if

therefore thine eye be single, thy whole
body shall be full of light.

But if thine eye be evil, thy whole
body shall be full of darkness. If therefore the light that is in thee be darkness,
how great is that darkness!

No man can serve two masters: for
either he will hate the one, and love the
other; or else he will hold to the one, and
despise the other. Ye cannot serve God
and mammon.

Therefore I say unto you, Take no
thought for your life, what ye shall eat,
or what ye shall drink; nor yet for your
body, what ye shall put on. Is not the
life more than meat, and the body than
raiment?

Behold the fowls of the air: for they
sow not, neither do they reap, nor gather
into barns; yet your heavenly Father
feedeth them? Are ye not much better
than they?

Which of you by taking thought can
add one cubit unto his stature?

And why take ye thought for raiment? Consider the lilies of the field.

how they grow; they toil not, neither do they spin:

And yet I say unto you, That even Solomon in all his glory was not arrayed like one of these.

Wherefore, if God so clothe the grass of the field, which to day is, and to morrow is cast into the oven, shall he not much more clothe you, O ye of little faith?

Therefore take no thought saying, What shall we eat? or, What shall we drink? or, Wherewithal shall we be clothed?

(For after all these things do the Gentilesseek:) for your heavenly Father knoweth that ye have need of all these things.

But seek ye first the kingdom of God, and his righteousness; and all these things shall be added unto you.

Take therefore no thought for the morrow: for the morrow shall take thought for the things of itself. Sufficient unto the day is the evil thereof.

JUDGE not, that ye be not judged.

For with what judgment ye judge, ye shall be judged: and with what measure ye mete, it shall be measured to you again.

And why beholdest thou the mote that is in thy brother's eye, but considerest not the beam that is in thine own eye?

Or how wilt thou say to thy brother, Let me pull out the mote out of thine eye; and, behold a beam is in thine own eye?

Thou hypocrite, first cast out the beam out of thine own eye; and then shalt thou see clearly to cast out the mote out of thy brother's eye.

Give not that which is holy unto the dogs, neither cast ye your pearls before swine, lest they trample them under their feet, and turn again and rend you.

Ask, and it shall be given you; seek, and ye shall find; knock, and it shall be opened unto you:

For every one that asketh receiveth; and he that seeketh findeth; and to him that knocketh it shall be opened.

Or what man is there of you, whom if his son ask bread, will he give him a stone?

Or if he ask a fish, will he give him a serpent?

If ye then, being evil, know how to give good gifts unto your children, how much more shall your Father which is in heaven give good things to them that ask him?

Therefore all things whatsoever ye would that men should do to you, do ye even so to them : for this is the law and the prophets.

Enter ye in at the strait gate : for wide is the gate, and broad is the way that leadeth to destruction, and many there be which go in thereat :

Because strait is the gate, and narrow is the way, which leadeth unto life, and few there be that find it.

Beware of false prophets. which come to you in sheep's clothing, but inwardly they are ravening wolves.

Ye shall know them by their fruits. Do men gather grapes of thorns, or figs of thistles ?

Even so every good tree bringeth forth good fruit; but a corrupt tree bringeth forth evil fruit.

A good tree cannot bring forth evil fruit, neither can a corrupt tree bring forth good fruit.

Every tree that bringeth not forth good fruit is hewn down, and cast into the fire.

Wherefore by their fruits ye shall know them.

Not every one that saith unto me, Lord, Lord, shall enter into the kingdom of heaven; but he that doeth the will of my Father which is in heaven.

Many will say to me in that day, Lord, Lord, have we not prophesied in thy name? and in thy name have cast out devils; and in thy name done many wonderful works?

And then will I profess unto them, I never knew you: depart from me, ye that work iniquity.

Therefore whosoever heareth these sayings of mine, and doeth them, I will liken him unto a wise man, which built his house upon a rock:

And the rain descended, and the floods came, and the winds blew, and beat upon that house; and it fell not: for it was founded upon a rock.

And every one that heareth these sayings of mine, and doeth them not, shall be likened unto a foolish man, which built his house upon the sand :

And the rain descended, and the floods came, and the winds blew, and beat upon that house; and it fell, and great was the fall of it.

And it came to pass, when Jesus had ended these sayings, the people were astonished at his doctrine :

For he taught them as one having authority, and not as the scribes.

The Discourse being ended, the following or some other suitable prayer may be offered.

GRANT, we beseech thee, Almighty God, that the words which we have heard this day with our outward ears, may, through thy grace, be so grafted inwardly in our hearts, that they may bring forth in us the fruit of good living, to the honor and praise of thy name; through Jesus Christ our Lord.

The grace of our Lord Jesus, and the love of God, and the communion of the Holy Ghost, be with us all evermore. Amen.

ADDITIONAL PRAYERS.

CONFESSIONS.

I.

WE sinners acknowledge before thee, our God and Creator, that we have grievously, and in manifold ways, sinned against thee, not only with outward transgression, but much more with inward blindness, unbelief, impatience, pride, hatred, and other sinful affections; as thou our Lord and God well knowest, and we, alas! cannot deeply enough deplore. But we repent of these things and are sorry for them, and heartily beseech thee for mercy, for the sake of thy beloved Son Jesus Christ our Lord.

II.

ALMIGHTY and most merciful Father; We have erred and strayed from thy ways like lost sheep. We

have followed too much the devices and
desires of our own hearts. We have
offended against thy holy laws. We
have left undone those things which we
ought to have done; and we have done
those things which we ought not to have
done; And there is no health in us.
But thou, O Lord, have mercy upon us
miserable offenders. Spare thou those,
O God, who confess their faults. Restore
thou those who are penitent; according
to thy promises declared unto mankind
in Christ Jesus our Lord. And grant, O
most merciful Father, for his sake, that
we may hereafter live a godly, righteous,
and sober life, to the glory of thy holy
name.

III.

O LORD God, Almighty and everlasting Father, we acknowledge and
confess before thy holy Majesty that we
are miserable sinners, born in iniquity,
prone to do evil, transgressing without
end thy holy commandments; Wherefore
we have drawn upon ourselves just con-

demnation and death. But we heartily
repent our offences; We condemn ourselves and our evil ways; We beseech
thee to relieve our distress. Have mercy
upon us, O Father of all mercies; and
grant us the daily increase of thy Holy
Spirit; that, being truly repentant, we
may turn from all sin, and hereafter live
to thine honor and glory.

IV.

ALMIGHTY God, Father of our Lord
Jesus Christ, Maker of all things
Judge of all men; we acknowledge and
bewail our manifold sins and wickedness,
which we, from time to time, most grievously have committed, by thought, word,
and deed, against thy divine majesty,
provoking most justly thy wrath and in-
dignation against us. We do earnestly
repent, and are heartily sorry for these
our misdoings. Have mercy upon us,
have mercy upon us, most merciful Father; for thy Son our Lord Jesus Christ's
sake, forgive us all that is past; and
grant that we may ever hereafter serve

and please thee in newness or life, to the honor and glory of thy name.

INVOCATIONS.

I.

ALMIGHTY God, who of thy great mercy hast gathered us into thy holy presence; grant that we may not swerve from the purity of thy worship; but so honor thee both in spirit and in outward forms, that thy name in us may be glorified, and we be indeed the members of thine only begotten Son Jesus Christ our Lord.

II.

O GOD, who art a Spirit, and wilt be worshipped in spirit and in truth, mercifully free us from the temptation of evil thoughts and base affections, that we may become a meet habitation of thy Holy Spirit, and serve thee with a pure devotion; through Jesus Christ our Lord.

III.

ALMIGHTY God, unto whom all hearts are open, all desires known,

and from whom no secrets are hid ; cleanse
the thoughts of our hearts by the inspira-
tion of thy Holy Spirit, that we may per-
fectly love thee, and worthily magnify
thy holy name; through Christ our Lord.

IV.

ALMIGHTY and everlasting God, who
hast commanded us to assemble ourselves together in the name of thy well-
beloved Son, and promised for his sake to
hear our prayers; mercifully regard thy
servants here gathered together according to thy will, and by the grace of thy
Holy Spirit, so lift up our thoughts and
draw forth our desires unto thee, that we
may render thee an holy, acceptable, and
reasonable service; through the merits of
Jesus Christ our Lord.

CONCLUDING PRAYERS.

I.

ALMIGHTY God, who sufferest none
that hope in thee to be afflicted over
much, but dost afford a gracious ear unto

their prayers, we render thee thanks for that thou hast heard our supplications and vows; and we most humbly beseech thee, that we may evermore be protected from all adversities; through Christ our Lord.

II.

WE beseech thee, O Lord, to graciously accept these our humble supplications and prayers, which we offer unto thee not in our own name or merits, but only in the blessed name and through the infinite merits of thy well-beloved Son Jesus Christ our Lord, who liveth and reigneth with thee and the Holy Ghost, ever one God, world without end.

III.

O GOD, whose mercies are without number, and the treasure of whose goodness is infinite; we render thee thanks for the gifts thou hast bestowed upon us, evermore beseeching thy compassion; that as thou grantest the petitions of them that faithfully ask thee, thou wilt never for-

sake them, but prepare them for the rewards to come, in thy everlasting kingdom.

IV.

ALMIGHTY God, who hast promised
to hear the petitions of them that
ask in thy Son's name; We beseech thee
mercifully to incline thine ear to us that
have made now our prayers and supplications unto thee; and grant, that these
things which we have faithfully asked according to thy will, may effectually be
obtained, to the relief of our necessity,
and to the setting forth of thy glory;
through Jesus Christ our Lord.   Amen.

A FORM OF DAILY PRAYERS

NATIONAL OR STATE LEGISLATURES.

The following prayers, or a portion of them, may be offered.

A Daily Prayer for Divine Mercy.

ALMIGHTY and everlasting God, who art always more ready to hear than we to pray, and art wont to give more than either we desire or deserve; pour down upon us the abundance of thy mercy, forgiving us those things whereof our conscience is afraid, and giving us those good things which we are not worthy to ask, but through the merits and mediation of Jesus Christ thy Son, our Lord.

A Daily Prayer for National (or State) Authorities.

O MOST powerful Lord God, King of kings, and Lord of lords, the blessed and only Potentate, who alone ordainest the powers that be; Take under thy most gracious government and guidance, we beseech thee, thy servants, the *President*, the *Judges*, and the *Congress* of the *United States*,* and all others in authority; and so enrich them with heavenly wisdom and grace, that they may attain thy everlasting favor, and we lead quiet and peaceable lives, in all godliness and honesty, through Jesus Christ our Lord.

A Daily Prayer for Divine Guidance.

To be used during a Session of Congress (or of a State Legislature.)

O GOD, who art the fountain of wisdom and lover of charity, from whom cometh every good and perfect gift, shed down upon these thy servants in council assembled, the spirit of concord, justice, and peace; that all their doings, being ordered by thy governance, may redound to the honor and welfare of the people, and to the glory of thy holy Name.

Here may be offered any of the *Sundry Prayers* or *Thanksgivings*, which may be requisite and fitting.

---

* In State Legislatures the form may be,—the *Governor, Legislature, and Magistrates of this Commonwealth.*

SEVERAL DAILY PRAYERS,

Any of which may be used as a Concluding Prayer.

For the Continuance of Divine Favors.

ALMIGHTY God, our heavenly Father, whose mercies are without number, and the treasure of whose goodness is infinite, we render thee thanks for all the gifts thou hast bestowed upon us; evermore beseeching thy compassion; that as thou grantest the petitions of them that faithfully ask thee, thou wilt never forsake them, but prepare them for the rewards to come, in thy everlasting kingdom; through Jesus Christ our Lord.

For a Gracious Answer to Prayers.

ALMIGHTY God, who hast promised to hear the petitions of them that ask in thy Son's name, we beseech thee mercifully to incline thine ears to us that have made now our prayers and supplication unto thee; and grant that those things which we have faithfully asked according to thy will, may effectually be obtained, to the relief of our necessity, and to the setting forth of thy glory, through Jesus Christ our Lord.

For Future Guidance.

ASSIST us mercifully, O Lord, in these our supplications and prayers, and dispose the way of thy servants towards the attainment of everlasting salvation, that among all the changes and chances of this mortal life, they may be defended by thy most gracious and ready help, through Jesus Christ our Lord.

The grace of our Lord Jesus Christ, and the love of God, and the communion of the Holy Ghost, be with us all evermore. Amen.

A FORM OF DAILY PRAYERS

SUITABLE TO BE USED IN

THE ARMY OF THE UNITED STATES.

After the reading of one of the Scripture Lessons or Psalms (see Table page 123), or the singing of a Hymn, the following Prayers, or a portion of them, may be offered:—

The Lord's Prayer.

OUR Father, who art in Heaven; Hallowed be thy name; Thy kingdom come; Thy will be done on earth as it is in heaven; Give us this day our daily bread; And forgive us our trespasses, as we forgive those who trespass against us; And lead us not into temptation; But deliver us from evil; for thine is the kingdom, and the power, and the glory, for ever and ever.

A Morning Prayer for Guidance.

O LORD, our heavenly Father, Almighty and everlasting God, who hast safely brought us to the beginning of this day; Defend us in the same by thy mighty power; and grant that this day we fall into no sin, neither run into any kind of danger; but that all our doings, being ordered by thy governance, may be righteous in thy sight, through Jesus Christ our Lord.

An Evening Prayer for Protection.

O LORD, our heavenly Father, by whose almighty power we have been preserved this day, by thy great mercy defend us from all perils of this night, for the love of thy only Son our Saviour Jesus Christ.

A Daily Prayer for Peace.

O GOD, who art the author of peace and lover of concord, in knowledge of whom standeth our eternal life, whose service is perfect freedom; Defend us thy humble servants in all assaults of our enemies; that we, surely trusting in thy defence, may not fear the power of any adversaries, through the might of Jesus Christ our Lord.

A Daily Prayer for the Civil Authorities of the United States.

ALMIGHTY and Eternal God, the blessed and only Potentate, King of kings and Lord of lords, who alone ordainest the powers that be; Take under thy most gracious government and guidance, we beseech thee, thy servants the *President*, the *Judges*, and the *Congress* of the *United States*, and all others in authority; and so enrich them with heavenly wisdom and grace, that they may attain thy everlasting favor, and we lead quiet and peaceable lives in all godliness and honesty, through Christ our Lord.

A Daily Prayer for the Army.

O LORD God, high and mighty, who doest thy will in the army of heaven and amongst the inhabitants of the earth; Stretch forth the shield of thy most merciful protection over us thy servants and the Army (or Regiment) in which we serve. Lead and guide us evermore by the counsel of thy goodness; Strengthen and defend us with thy might; that we

7

may steadfastly continue an honor and bulwark of our land, a terror to evil doers, and a sure defence against every enemy; and finally, having quitted ourselves like men, and as good soldiers of the Lord Jesus, may enter into thy eternal glory, through Him who is our only Deliverer and the Captain of our salvation, Jesus Christ our Lord.

Here may be offered any of the Sundry Prayers which may be requisite. (See pages 61—73.)

A Daily Prayer to the God of Battles.

To be used during a campaign.

O MOST powerful and glorious Lord God, the Lord of hosts and God of battles, who alone sittest in the throne judging right, and givest not alway the battle to the strong, but canst save by many or by few; We, thy poor servants, do make our humble appeal to Thee, in this our extremity, that thou wouldst take the cause into thine own hand and judge between us and our enemies. Arise, O Lord, and come and help us. Let not our sins now cry against us for vengeance, nor our iniquities give thine heritage to reproach; but cover thou our heads, O God, in the day of battle as with thy shield, and by thine own right arm bring us the victory; through Jesus Christ our Lord.

SEVERAL DAILY PRAYERS,

Any of which may be used in concluding Morning or Evening Prayers.

I.

For a Blessing upon Daily Labors.

DIRECT us, O Lord, in all our doings, with thy most gracious favor, and further us with thy continual help; that in all our works, begun. continued, and ended in thee, we may glorify thy holy Name; and finally, by thy mercy, obtain everlasting life; through Jesus Christ our Lord.

II.

For Grace to perform Daily Duties.

O ALMIGHTY Lord, and everlasting God, vouchsafe, we beseech thee, to direct, sanctify, and govern both our hearts and bodies, in the ways of thy laws, and in the works of thy commandments; that through thy most mighty protection, both here and ever, we may be preserved in body and soul; through our Lord and Saviour Jesus Christ.

III.

For Future Guidance.

ASSIST us mercifully, O Lord, in these our supplications and prayers, and dispose the way of thy servants towards the attainment of everlasting salvation; that among all the changes and chances of this mortal life we may ever be defended by thy most gracious and ready help; through Jesus Christ our Lord.

IV.

For a Gracious Answer to Prayers.

ALMIGHTY God, the Fountain of all wisdom, who knowest our necessities before we ask, and our ignorance in asking; We beseech thee to have compassion upon our infirmities; and those things which for our unworthiness we dare not, and for our blindness we cannot ask, vouchsafe to give us, for the worthiness of thy son Jesus Christ our Lord.

The grace of our Lord Jesus Christ, and the love of God, and the communion of the Holy Ghost, be with us all evermore. Amen.

A FORM OF DAILY PRAYERS

SUITABLE TO BE USED IN

THE NAVY OF THE UNITED STATES.

After the reading of one of the Scripture Lessons or Psalms (see Table, page 123,) or the singing of a Hymn, the following Prayers, or a portion of them, may be offered :—

The Lord's Prayer.

OUR Father, who art in heaven; Hallowed be thy name; Thy kingdom come; Thy will be done on earth as it is in heaven; Give us this day our daily bread; And forgive us our trespasses as we forgive those who trespass against us; And lead us not into temptation; But deliver us from evil ; For thine is the kingdom, and the power, and the glory, for ever and ever.

A Morning Prayer for Guidance.

O LORD, our Heavenly Father, Almighty and everlasting God, who hast safely brought us to the beginning of this day; Defend us in the same with thy mighty power; and grant that this day we fall into no sin, neither run into any kind of danger; but that all our doings being ordered by thy governance, may be righteous in thy sight; through Jesus Christ our Lord.

An Evening Prayer for Protection.

LIGHTEN our darkness we beseech thee, O Lord; and by thy great mercy defend us from all perils and dangers of this night; for the love of thy only son our Saviour Jesus Christ.

A Daily Prayer for Security.

O GOD, from whom all holy desires, all good counsels, and all just works do proceed; give unto thy servants that peace, which the world cannot give; that our hearts may be set to obey thy commandments, and also that by thee, we, being defended from the fear of our enemies, may pass our time in rest and quietness; through the merits of Jesus Christ our Lord. Amen.

A Daily Prayer for the Civil Authorities of the United States.

ALMIGHTY and Eternal God, King of kings and Lord of lords, the blessed and only Potentate, who alone ordainest the Powers that be; take under thy most gracious government and guidance, we beseech thee, thy servants the *President*, the *Judges*, and the *Congress* of the *United States*, and all others in authority; and so enrich them with heavenly wisdom and grace, that both they may attain thy everlasting favor, and we lead quiet and peaceable lives in all godliness and honesty; through Christ our Lord.

A Daily Prayer to be used in the Navy.

O ETERNAL Lord God, who alone spreadest out the heavens and rulest the raging of the sea, and hast compassed the waters with bounds until day and night come to an end; be pleased to receive into thy Almighty and most gracious protection the persons of us thy servants, and the Fleet (or Ship) in which we serve. Preserve us from the dangers of the deep and from the violence of enemies; that we may be a safeguard unto our country, and a security for such as do business in the mighty waters; that the inhabitants of our land may have peace and freedom to serve thee; and that in due season we may return to our homes, with a thankful remembrance of thy mercies; and, finally, having passed the sea of this troublous life, may enter the haven of eternal rest, through Him, who is our only refuge and Saviour, Jesus Christ our Lord.

Here may be offered any of the Sundry Prayers which the circumstances require.

A Daily Prayer to the God of Battles,
To be used during a campaign.

O MOST powerful and glorious Lord God, the Lord of hosts and God of battles, who alone sittest on the throne judging right, and givest not alway the battle to the strong, but canst save by many or by few; We thy poor servants, make our humble appeal to thy divine majesty, in this our extremity, that thou wouldst take the cause into thine own hand and judge between us and our enemies. Arise, O Lord, and come and help us. Let not our sins now cry against us for vengeance, nor our iniquities give thine heritage to reproach; but cover thou our heads, O God, in the day of battle as with thy shield, and by thine own right arm bring us the victory; through Jesus Christ our Lord.

SEVERAL DAILY PRAYERS,

Any one of which may be used in concluding Morning or Evening Prayers.

I.

For Divine Grace in Daily Duties.

O ALMIGHTY Lord and everlasting God, vouchsafe, we beseech thee, to direct, sanctify, and govern both our hearts and bodies, in the ways of thy laws and in the works of thy commandments; that through thy most mighty protection, both here and ever, we may be preserved in body and soul; through our Lord and Saviour Jesus Christ.

II.

For a Blessing upon Daily Labors.

DIRECT us, O Lord, in all our doings
with thy most gracious favor, and
further us with thy continual help; that
in all our works begun, continued, and
ended in thee, we may glorify thy holy
name, and finally by thy mercy obtain
everlasting life, through Jesus Christ our
Lord.

III.

For Future Guidance.

ASSIST us mercifully, O Lord, in
these our supplications and prayers,
and dispose the way of thy servants towards the attainment of everlasting salvation; that among all the changes and
chances of this mortal life, they may ever
be defended by thy most gracious and
ready help; through Jesus Christ our
Lord.

IV.

For a Gracious Answer to Prayers.

ALMIGHTY God, who hast promised
to hear the petitions of them that
ask in thy Son's name; we beseech thee

mercifully to incline thine ears to us
that have made now our prayers and supplications unto thee; and grant that those
things which we have faithfully asked
according to thy will, may effectually be
obtained, to the relief of our necessity,
and to the setting forth of thy glory;
through Jesus Christ our Lord.

THE grace of Our Lord Jesus Christ,
and the love of God, and the Communion of the Holy Ghost be with us all
evermore.   Amen.

SUNDRY PUBLIC PRAYERS AND THANKSGIVINGS.

PRAYERS.

For Health.

DEFEND us, O Lord, from all perils of mind and body, and for the love of thy only Son our Saviour, grant us health and peace; that, all erroneous and hurtful things being averted from us, we may serve thee with a sound body and please thee with a clean heart; through Christ our Lord.

For the Sick.

ALMIGHTY and most merciful Father, the everlasting refuge of thy believing children, hear us for thy sick servants, whom it hath pleased thee to afflict with bodily disease and weakness, and mercifully comfort and relieve them, that health returning to them thanks may be returned to thee; through Jesus Christ our Lord.

6

For the Dying.

O MOST merciful and gracious Lord God, who didst give thine only begotten Son Jesus Christ that whosoever believeth on him might not perish but have eternal life; Look down in mercy, we beseech thee, upon those thy servants who are nigh unto death, and, for the glory of thy compassion, be pleased to enlighten, pardon, and comfort them, that whensoever released from this mortal body, their souls may be presented to thee, their Creator, without spot of sin; through the cleansing blood of their only Saviour, Jesus Christ our Lord.

After Instances of Mortality.

O GOD, whose days are without end and whose mercies cannot be numbered, make us, we beseech thee, deeply sensible of the shortness and uncertainty of life, and of the speedy coming of death and judgment; and by these daily instances of mortality, teach us to apply ourselves unto wisdom; that so among the sundry and manifold changes of the world, our hearts may surely be there fixed where true joys are to be found; through Jesus Christ our Lord.

On Commencing a Journey or March.

O MOST glorious Lord God, who of old didst lead thine armies as with a pillar of cloud by day and of fire by night, be our Leader and Guardian, we beseech thee, in all our journeyings; our support in setting out; our solace on the way; our shadow in the heat; our covert in the rain and cold; the chariot of our weariness; the fortress of our adversity; and our staff in the ways of slipperiness; that under thy guidance we may safely come to our journey's end, and at length to the end of this our earthly warfare and pilgrimage; through Jesus Christ our Lord.

On Commencing a Voyage.

O MOST powerful Lord God, who didst carry the hosts of Israel through the sea, singing the praise of thy name, let thy grace going before and attending on our voyage, find for us a pathway upon the waters, and be to us our solace in setting sail; our guiding star on the way; our wand of peace among tempests; the shield of our defence against enemies; our harbor in shipwreck; and the anchor of our hope; that so we may come at length to the desired haven, both in this life and in the life immortal; through Jesus Christ our Lord.

For Friends at Home.

O LORD, our heavenly Father, bless and keep, we pray thee, our kindred, friends, and benefactors, and graciously watch between them and us while we are absent one from another, that in due time we may meet again to praise thee, and hereafter dwell together in heavenly mansions; through Christ our Lord.

Among Temptations.

O GOD, who knowest us to be set in the midst of so many and great dangers that by reason of the frailty of our nature we cannot always stand upright; grant to us such strength and protection as may support us in all dangers, and carry us through all temptations; through Jesus Christ our Lord.

During Scarcity of Food.

ALMIGHTY and most merciful Creator, who openest thy hand to the wants of every living thing, and feedest even the young ravens when they cry; leave us not, we beseech thee, to perish for the lack of that without which we cannot live to praise thee, but out of thy bounty mercifully relieve our necessity; through Jesus Christ our Lord.

For Rain.

O GOD, in whom we live, and move, and have our being, grant to us seasonable rain and heavenly showers; that being refreshed in things temporal we may the more faithfully seek after things eternal; through Christ our Lord.

For Fair Weather.

HEAR thy suppliant children, O Lord, crying unto thee, and by thy clemency restrain the flood of waters and bestow upon us fair weather and heavenly sunshine, that through the clouds of thy judgment we may still behold the light of thy mercy; through Christ our Lord.

In Storms at Sea.

O MOST glorious and gracious Lord God, who dwellest in heaven, but beholdest all things below; look down, we beseech thee, and hear us, calling out of the depth of misery, and out of the jaws of this death, which is ready now to swallow us up: Save, Lord, or we perish. The living—the living shall praise thee. O send thy word of command to rebuke the raging winds and the roaring sea; that we, being delivered from this distress, may live to serve thee, and glorify thy name all the days of our life; through the infinite merits of our blessed Saviour, thy Son our Lord Jesus Christ.

Among Enemies on Land or at Sea.

DEFEND us, O Lord, in all assaults of our enemies, and powerfully rescue us from their snares, that we may not be cast down for our sins, but for thy mercy

give thee unceasing thanks; through Christ
our Lord.

For Charity towards Enemies.

ALMIGHTY God, our heavenly Father, who causest thy sun to rise on
the evil and on the good, and sendest rain
on the just and on the unjust; make us
partakers, we beseech thee, of thy divine
compassion toward all that offend and
harm us, and plenteously endue them
with charity and peace, that both they
and we may obtain thy mercy; through
Jesus Christ our Lord.

For those taken Prisoners.

O MOST gracious God, our refuge in
every trouble, we humbly beseech
thee to guard and cherish those thy servants, whom it hath pleased thee to deliver
into the hands of our enemies, and by thy
favor lighten their durance and loosen
their bonds, that speedily they may give
thee thanks for a marvellous deliverance;
through Christ Jesus our Lord.

For the Wounded.

LOOK down, O Lord, in tender love and pity, upon these thy suffering children, grievously afflicted with the blows and hurts of a bitter warfare, and be pleased, as with the oil and wine of thy healthful grace, to sooth their pains, bind up their wounds, and renew their strength; for the glory of thy mercy; through Christ our Lord.

For those under Sentence of Death.

O GOD, who declarest thy almighty power chiefly in showing mercy and pity; we beseech thee to have mercy upon thy servants who for their transgressions are appointed to die. Grant that they may take thy judgments patiently and repent them truly of their sins; that, recovering thy favor, the fearful reward of their actions may end with this life; and whensoever their souls shall depart from the body, they may be without spot presented to thee; through Jesus Christ our Lord.

After a Disaster of Arms.

O RIGHTEOUS God, and most merciful Father, who hast seen fit to appoint us unto reproach and misery at the hands of our enemies; grant us grace, we beseech thee, to humble ourselves under thy chastenings, with courage, faith, and hope, in this day of our adversity; that though cast down we may not be destroyed, but rise again through thy help, and in thy strength still become conquerors, and more than conquerors; through him that loved us, Christ Jesus our Lord.

On Entering an Engagement.

A LMIGHTY God, our Maker, Judge, and Saviour, from whom our spirits have come, to whom they shall return; we thy sinful creatures; humbly confessing all our sins; meekly begging thy forgiveness; desiring charity with all men; praying for thy mighty help, and putting our whole trust in thee; do commend ourselves into thy hands; through Jesus Christ our Lord.

The grace of our Lord Jesus Christ,

the love of God our Father, and the fellowship of the Holy Ghost be with us all for evermore. Amen.

THANKSGIVINGS.

For the Recovery of the Sick and Wounded.

O LORD God. who both healest by wounding and preservest by pardoning, we give thee hearty thanks for these thy servants, raised up in thy marvellous mercy from the bed of sickness and the jaws of death; and we humbly beseech thee, that both with their bodies and their souls, which thou hast delivered. they may evermore faithfully serve thee; through Jesus Christ our Lord.

For Supplies of Food.

ACCEPT our thanks, O Lord, for that thou hast heard our prayers, and turned our dearth and scarcity into plenty; and grant, we beseech thee, that even as we ever live upon thy bounty, so we may ever live for thine honor and glory; through Christ our Lord.

For Returning Rain.

BLESSED Lord, who at length hast opened the windows of heaven and rained down upon us these drops and showers of mercy; grant that what we praise and magnify as an earthly refreshment, may be to us also a heavenly benediction; through Christ our Lord.

For Deliverance from Storms.

O MOST merciful and mighty God, who at thy pleasure raisest the winds and waves of the sea, or commandest them back to peace, we thy poor creatures, spared by thy mercy to praise thee, do give thee unfeigned thanks, for that thou heardest our cry when we were at the brink of death and had given up all for lost, and didst not suffer us to sink in the devouring waters: And we here offer ourselves, our bodies and our souls, which thou hast redeemed, to be a living sacrifice unto thee, of praise and thanksgiving, all the days of our lives; through Jesus Christ our Lord.

For Deliverance from Enemies.

O ALMIGHTY God, who art a strong tower of defence unto thy servants against the face of their enemies, we yield thee praise and thanksgiving for our deliverance from those great and apparent dangers wherewith we were compassed; we acknowledge it thy goodness that we were not delivered over as a prey unto them; beseeching thee still to continue such thy mercies towards us, that all the world may know that thou art our Saviour and mighty Deliverer, through Jesus Christ our Lord.

For Safe Return of Prisoners.

A LMIGHTY and most merciful God, who in times of old didst loosen the chains of thy believing servants, and let them depart unhurt from the midst of their enemies; we praise and magnify that preserving mercy whereby these thy servants, brought back from captivity, are here before thee, to thank and bless thee as their Guardian and Deliverer; through Jesus Christ our Lord.

For Safe Return from a Campaign or Voyage.

ALL thanks and praise be unto thee, O most glorious God, our good and gracious Father, who in thy wondrous power and mercy hast preserved us thy servants through so many and great dangers, temptations and troubles; guiding and guarding us, by night and by day; in heat and cold, on land and water; through hunger and thirst and weariness; among enemies; and in the midst of battle and murder and death. Surely goodness and mercy have followed us until this hour; and therefore we will not forget thy benefits, but pay our vows unto thee, and call upon our souls and all that is within us to bless and magnify thy holy name; through Jesus Christ our Lord.

5

A FORM OF PUBLIC HUMILIATION.

SUITED TO

FAST DAYS APPOINTED BY CIVIL AUTHORITIES.

The usual order of Divine service may be observed, with the substitution of such parts as here follow :

Introductory Sentences.

WHEREWITH shall we come before the Lord and bow ourselves before the High God? Behold he putteth no trust in his saints; yea, the heavens are not clean in his sight. How much more abominable and filthy is man which drinketh iniquity like water.

We will set our faces unto the Lord God, to seek by prayer and supplications, with fasting and sackcloth and ashes : We will pray unto the Lord our God and make our confession; Who can tell if God will repent, and turn away from us his fierce anger that we perish not?

A General Confession of Public Sins.

O MOST mighty God, terrible in thy judgments and wonderful in thy doings towards the children of men; we thy sinful creatures here assembled before thee, do on behalf of the whole people of this land, humbly confess the manifold sins, both of ourselves and of our rulers, whereby we have drawn down upon us thy righteous displeasure. Guilty! Guilty! Guilty! O Lord, are we all before thee this day. But enter not, O Lord, into judgment with thy servants, seeing that in thy sight can none living be justified; neither visit upon posterity the reward of our transgressions. Be merciful, O Lord, be merciful unto thy people whom thou hast redeemed, and be not angry with us forever; but pardon us for thy mercy's sake; through the merits of thy son Jesus Christ our Lord.

For suitable Psalms, Scripture Lessons, and Hymns see Tables, pages 130–132.

PRAYERS

To be used as the occasion requires.

A Prayer in times of Public Calamity.

O ALMIGHTY God, who desirest not the death but the life of sinners, despise not thy people returning unto thee in their affliction, but for the glory of thy name be pleased to hear and succor us; that the hearts of men may know that these scourges proceed from thy justice and cease by thy mercy; through Christ our Lord.

A Prayer in time of Pestilence.

HOLY Lord God Almighty, who of old didst stay the angel of pestilence at the cry of thy repenting children, and bring back health to a dying people; hear us, thy suppliants, returning to thee, as in sackcloth, dust and ashes, and mercifully lift from us the heavy hand of thy righteous visitation; that the people may live before thee, and not die in their sins, and that the land may no longer mourn by reason of thy judgments, O Lord, who for our iniquities art justly displeased.

7*

A Prayer in time of Drought or Famine.

O GOD, our Creator, Preserver, and Bountiful Benefactor, who givest seed time and harvest, and sendest both the early and latter rain; have pity, we beseech thee, upon thy famished people who cry unto thee in their tribulation, and in thy compassion return and visit us; that the heavens may no longer be as brass above, and the earth as iron beneath, to shut out from us thy mercy, but that all the people may praise thee, O God, who art the Fountain of living waters and the Father of mercies, from whom cometh down every good and perfect gift; through Jesus Christ our Lord.

A Prayer in time of War.

O MOST wise and righteous God, King of all nations, and Judge of the whole earth, who by wars and fightings art pleased to scourge the ungodly and vindicate the just; aid us, thy servants, we beseech thee, who, in this our cause and warfare do put our whole trust in thee, and by thy mercy save and deliver us from the hands

of our enemies; that we, being armed
with thy defence, may be preserved evermore from all perils, to glorify thee, who
art the only giver of victory; through the
merits of thy only Son, Jesus Christ our
Lord.

A Prayer during Insurrections and Tumults.

O ALMIGHTY Lord God, who alone
riddest away the tyrants of this
world by thine everlasting determination,
and stillest the noise and tumult of the
people; stir up thy great strength, we beseech thee, and come and help us, and by
the breath of thy vengeance scatter the
counsels of them that secretly devise mischief, and bring thou their violent dealings to nought; that the land may have
rest before thee, and that all the people
may praise thee, O God, who only hast
been our Deliverer, and only canst be
our Help and our Shield, both now and
evermore.

A Prayer for Armies in the Field.

A LMIGHTY God, the Saviour of all
men, we humbly commend to thy tender care and sure protection, thy servants

who have gone forth at the call of their country to defend its government, and to protect us in our property and homes. Let thy fatherly hand, we beseech thee, be over them; let thy Holy Spirit be with them; let thy good angels have charge of them; with thy loving kindness defend them as with a shield, and either bring them out of their peril in safety, with a heart to show forth thy praises for ever, or else sustain them with that glorious hope, by which alone thy servants can have victory in suffering and death; through the sole merits of Jesus Christ our Lord.

A Prayer for Rulers and People in Troublous Times.

OH! most mighty God! King of kings and Lord of lords, without whose care the watchman waketh but in vain, we implore, in this our time of need, thy succor and blessing in behalf of our rulers and magistrates, and of all the people of this land. Remember not our many and great transgressions; turn from us the judgments which we feel, and the yet greater judgments which we fear; and give us wisdom to discern, and faithfulness to do, and patience to endure, whatsoever shall be well-pleasing in thy sight; that so thy chastenings may yield the peaceful fruits of righteousness, and that at the last, we may rejoice in thy salvation.; through Jesus Christ our Lord.

A Prayer for the Preservation of the United States.

O ALMIGHTY Lord, governor of all men, and God of our fathers, who hast brought forth this people from the midst of the nations with a mighty and outstretched arm, and established us in peace and freedom, and knit us together in one blessed union of states, churches, and kindreds; most humbly we beseech thee ever more keep us the same, through all assaults and dangers, against every gathering together of the froward, and every uprising of evil doers; that no secret conspiracies nor open violences may distract or divide us; but that, being surrounded by thy might, and clinging together under the shadow of thy wings, we may steadfastly continue, one and inseparable, now and forever, for the honor and welfare of our country, for the good of mankind, and for the glory of thy holy Name.

A Prayer for the Return of Peace.

O GOD, guardian of peace and lover of charity, stretch forth the wings of thy compassion over thy stricken people, and let heavenly peace return throughout our borders; that, being no longer shaken with terrors, we may employ thy tranquility for the remedy of our faults and for the recovery of thy favor; through Jesus Christ our Lord.

A Prayer for the Removal of all Evils.

ALMIGHTY and everlasting God, whose power is unchangeable and light eternal, mercifully regard the wonderful mystery of thy whole church, and silently work the work of human salvation by thine unchanging purpose, until the whole world shall experience and see the downcast raised, the decayed renewed, and all things return to their perfection, by the might of that Spirit from whom they took their beginning; through Christ our Lord.

A FORM OF PUBLIC THANKS-GIVING.

SUITED TO DAYS APPOINTED BY CIVIL AUTHO-RITIES.

The usual order of Divine Service may be observed, with the substitution of such parts as here follow :—

Introductory Sentences.

WHAT shall we render unto the Lord for all his benefits towards us ?

We will take the cup of salvation and call upon the name of the Lord; We will offer to him the sacrifice of thanksgiving; We will pay our vows unto the Lord now in the presence of all his people.

An Acknowledgment of Public Mercies.

O LORD God, King of saints and Judge of nations, who hast been exceedingly gracious unto this land, and by thy marvellous Providence crowned the year with loving-kindness, giving us ever of thy bounty all good things richly to enjoy; we thy creatures and subjects are

here before thee, with due thankfulness
to acknowledge, for ourselves and for all
the people, these thine unspeakable mercies, and to offer unto thee our sacrifice
of praise for the same; humbly beseeching thee to accept this our unfeigned
though unworthy oblation, and vowing all
holy obedience in thought, word and
work unto thee, who art our only King and
Sovereign, and our gracious Benefactor;
through Jesus Christ our Lord.

For suitable Psalms, Scripture Lessons and Hymns,
see Tables, pages 130–132.

THANKSGIVINGS

To be used as the occasion requires.

A Thanksgiving for American Independence.

ALMIGHTY God, who hast made of
one blood all nations of men to dwell
on all the face of the earth, and hast de-
termined the times before appointed, and
the bounds of their habitation; We yield
thee our unfeigned thanks and praise for
the wonderful and mighty deliverance
whereby thou didst raise up the people of
these United States from dependence and

distress to a name and a place among the nations, and give to them this good land for an inheritance. Not by our might or for our merit, but of thy goodness and through thy power and providence we are what we are this day before thee; and therefore not unto us, O Lord, not unto us, but unto thy name be ascribed all honor and glory, from generation to generation; through Jesus Christ our Lord.

A Thanksgiving for the Bounties of Providence.

O GOD, Giver of all good and Fountain of mercies, in whom are the springs of our life; all glory, thanks and praise be unto thee for thine ever and overflowing goodness; for thy faithfulness which is from one generation to another; for thy mercies which are new every morning, fresh every moment, and more than we can number; for seed time and harvest, and summer and winter, and nights and days throughout the year; for food and raiment and shelter; for health and reason; for childhood and age, and youth and manhood; for thy fatherly

8

hand ever upon us in sickness and in
health, in joy and in sorrow, in life and
in death; for friends and kindred and
kind benefactors; for home and country;
for thy church and for thy gospel; yea,
Lord, for that there is nothing for which
we may not bless and thank thee; And
therefore do we take the cup of salvation
and call upon thy name and pay our vows
now in the presence of all thy people;
humbly beseeching thee to accept this our
becoming service and bounden duty, even
as we offer it, in the name and through
the infinite merits of thy Son Jesus Christ
our Lord.

A Thanksgiving after the Removal of Pestilence.

O LORD God of our salvation, who
turnest man to destruction and say-
est, Return, ye children of men; We
yield thee hearty thanks for that thou didst
not shut the ears of thy mercy when we
cried unto thee, in the day of thy terrible
visitation, as out of the valley and shadow
of death; but hast mercifully driven from
our borders the wasting pestilence, and

restored the voice of joy and health into our dwellings. Of thy mercy it is, O Lord, that we were not utterly consumed and wasted away; and, therefore, as the living from the dead, we return to bless and praise and magnify thee; through Jesus Christ our Lord.

A Thanksgiving after the Removal of Famine.

WE yield thee abounding thanks, O most bountiful God and Father, who hast had compassion upon the multitudes that were ready to perish with hunger; and even as thou didst make the few loaves and fishes enough for thousands, art now crowning the seed time with harvest and filling the land with plenty. And we beseech thee, that unto this thy miracle of earthly Providence, thou wilt add thy richer miracle of heavenly grace, and evermore give us that bread which cometh down from heaven, whereof they that eat shall be nourished unto life eternal; through Jesus Christ our Lord.

A Thanksgiving for Victory over Enemies.

O ALMIGHTY God, the Sovereign Commander of all the world, in whose hands is power and might which none is able to withstand; We bless and magnify thy great and glorious name for the happy victory wherewith thou hast crowned our arms, and the whole glory whereof we do ascribe unto thee, the only Giver of victory. And, we beseech thee, give us grace to improve this great mercy to thy glory, the honor of our country, and, as much as in us lieth, to the good of all mankind; through Jesus Christ our Lord, to whom with thee and the Holy Spirit, as for all thy mercies, so in particular for this, be all glory and honor, world without end.

A Thanksgiving for the Restoration of Peace at Home.

O ETERNAL God, our heavenly Father, who alone makest men to be of one mind in a house, and stillest the outrage of a violent and unruly people; We bless thy holy name that it hath pleased thee to appease the seditious tumults which have been lately raised up among us; most humbly beseeching thee to grant to all of us grace, that we may henceforth obediently walk in thy holy commandments; and, leading a quiet and peaceable life in all godliness and honesty, may continually offer unto thee our sacrifice of praise and thanksgiving for these thy mercies toward us; through Jesus Christ our Lord.

A Thanksgiving for the Restoration of Peace Abroad.

ALMIGHTY and everlasting God, who makest wars to cease unto the ends of the earth, we praise and magnify that great mercy, whereby thou hast not only freed our borders from every enemy, and given us rest and quietness, but out of thine abundant goodness art shedding down the same blessed tranquility upon the nations round about us; and we humbly beseech thee that, being subdued by thy truth, they may evermore dwell together in love as one family of mankind; through Jesus Christ our Lord.

A Thanksgiving for the Promise of Millenium.

O MOST powerful Lord God, according to whose exceeding great and precious promises all the kingdoms of the world shall yet become the kingdom of thy Son our Lord, and the whole earth be filled with his glory, we give thee thanks for that blessed hope and certain prospect; beseeching thee, even now, to accept the ministry of our humble praises, as in concert with that innumerable multitude of all nations and kindreds and peoples and tongues, who together join in ascribing unto thee glory and honor, and majesty and power, and might and dominion, forever and ever. Amen.

A FORM OF FUNERAL SERVICE.

In ordinary cases, only the *Service at the Burial* (see page 102) need be used; but when public solemnities are to be conducted with a Funeral Discourse or Address, then the first part of the ensuing Form also may be used.

SERVICE BEFORE THE BURIAL.

In funeral solemnities, before proceeding to the place of burial, Lessons and Psalms, selected from the Tables, (see page 131,) may be read; or one or more of the following collections of Scripture Sentences may be read, as the occasion requires.

On any Funeral Occasion.

IT is better to go to the house of mourning than to go to the house of feasting, for that is the end of all men, and the living will lay it to his heart.

Lord, make me to know mine end, and the measure of my days, what it is; that I may know how frail I am. For I know that thou wilt bring me to death, and to the house appointed for all living.

What man is he that liveth and shall

not see death? shall he deliver his soul
from the hand of the grave? One dieth
in his full strength, being wholly at ease
and quiet; another dieth in the bitterness
of his soul, and never eateth with pleasure: they shall lie down alike in the
dust, and the worms shall cover them.
All flesh shall perish together, and man
shall turn again unto dust.

There is hope of a tree, if it be cut
down, that it will sprout again, and that
the tender branch thereof will not cease.
Though the root thereof wax old in the
earth, and the stock thereof die in the
ground: yet through the scent of water
it will bud, and bring forth boughs like a
plant. But man dieth and wasteth away;
yea man giveth up the ghost, and where
is he? As the waters fail from the sea,
and the flood decayeth and drieth up: so
man lieth down and riseth not: till the
heavens be no more, they shall not awake;
nor be raised out of their sleep.

If a man die, shall he live again? Jesus
said unto Martha, I am the Resurrection
and the life: he that believeth in me,

though he were dead, yet shall he live. And whosoever liveth and believeth in me shall never die.

It is appointed unto men once to die, but after this the judgment. We must all appear before the judgment seat of Christ, that every one may receive the things done in his body, according to that he hath done whether it be good or bad. If the tree fall toward the south, or toward the north, in the place where the tree falleth, there it shall be. He that is unjust, let him be unjust still; and he that is filthy, let him be filthy still; and he that is righteous, let him be righteous still; and he that is holy, let him be holy still.

The righteous hath hope in his death : Let me die the death of the righteous and let my last end be like his. Precious in the sight of the Lord is the death of his saints; The day of their death is better than that of their birth.

For we know that if our earthly house of this tabernacle be dissolved, we have a building of God, an house not made with

hands, eternal, in the heavens. There
the wicked cease from troubling, and the
weary are at rest. And they shall hunger no more, neither thirst any more;
neither shall the sun light on them, nor
any heat. And there shall be no more
death, neither sorrow, nor crying; neither
shall there be any more pain; for the
former things are passed away. And
God shall wipe away all tears from their
eyes.

On any Funeral Occasion.

MAN that is born of a woman is of few
days and full of trouble: He cometh
forth like a flower and is cut down; he
fleeth also as a shadow and continueth not.

When he dieth he shall carry nothing
away: his glory shall not descend after
him. As he came forth from his mother's
womb, naked shall he return to go as he
came, and he shall take nothing of his
labor which he may carry away in his
hand. We brought nothing into this
world and it is certain we can carry nothing out.

What is your life? It is even a vapor which appeareth for a little time and then vanisheth away. Our days on the earth are as a shadow, and there is none abiding. We spend our years as a tale that is told. The days of our years are threescore years and ten; and if, by reason of strength, they be fourscore years, yet is their strength labor and sorrow for it is soon cut off and we fly away. We all do fade as a leaf, and our iniquities like the wind have taken us away.

Boast not thyself of to-morrow; for thou knowest not what a day may bring forth. For man also knoweth not his time: as the fishes that are taken in an evil net, and as the birds that are caught in the snare; so are the sons of men snared in an evil time, when it falleth suddenly upon them. O my God, take me not away in the midst of my days, for I am a stranger with thee, and a sojourner as all my fathers were. O spare me that I may recover strength before I go hence and be no more.

But this I say, brethren, the time is

short; It remaineth that they that weep be as though they wept not; and they that rejoice, as though they rejoiced not; and they that buy, as though they possessed not; and they that use this world as not abusing it: for the fashion of this world passeth away.

Work while the day lasts; seeing that the night cometh wherein no man can work. Whatsoever thy hand findeth to do, do it with thy might; for there is no work, nor device, nor wisdom, nor knowledge in the grave whither thou goest.

At the Funeral of a Public Personage.

KNOW ye not that there is a prince and a great man fallen this day in Israel?

Behold the Lord, the Lord of Hosts, doth take away from Jerusalem and from Judah the stay and the staff, the whole stay of bread and the whole stay of water, the mighty man and the man of war, the judge and the prophet, and the prudent and the ancient, the captain of fifty, and the honorable man and the counsellor, and the cunning artificer, and the eloquent orator.

For wise men die, likewise the fool and the brutish person perish, and leave their wealth to others. They are exalted for a little while, but are gone and brought low; they are taken out of the way as all other, and cut off as the tops of the ears of corn.

Is it fit to say to a king, Thou art wicked? and to princes, Ye are ungodly? How much less to Him that accepteth not the persons of princes, nor regardeth the rich more than the poor? for they are all the work of his hands. In a moment shall they die, and the people shall be troubled at midnight, and pass away; and the mighty shall be taken away without hand.

Cease ye from man, whose breath is in his nostrils; for wherein is he to be accounted of?

At the Funeral of a Military Personage.

HOW are the mighty fallen, and the weapons of war perished! The beauty of Israel is slain upon thy high places: How are the mighty fallen!

The voice said, Cry. And he said,

What shall I cry? All flesh is grass, and all the goodliness thereof is as the flower of the field. Verily, every man at his best estate is altogether vanity.

This is an evil among all things that are done under the sun, that there is one event unto all. There is no man that hath power over the spirit to retain the spirit; neither hath he power in the day of death; and there is no discharge in that war.

If in this life only we have hope in Christ, we are of all men most miserable. But now is Christ risen from the dead, and become the first fruits of them which slept. When Christ, who is our life, shall appear, then shall ye also appear with Him in Glory. The grass withereth, the flower fadeth; but the Word of our God shall stand forever.

Yet a little while, and He that shall come, will come, and will not tarry. And He shall judge among the nations, and shall rebuke many people: and they shall beat their swords into ploughshares, and their spears into pruning-hooks; nation shall not lift up sword against nation, neither shall they learn war any more.

After the Funeral Discourse or Address, the following prayers, or a portion of them, may be offered.

A Prayer for Resignation.

O LORD God, our Heavenly Father, who alone art the author and the disposer of our life, from whom our spirits have come and to whom they shall return; we acknowledge thy sovereign power and right both to give and to take away, as seemeth good in thy sight; and we most humbly beseech thee, that unto all thy righteous dealings we may yield ourselves with due resignation and patience; being assured that though we understand not the mystery of thy ways, yet always in faithfulness, O Lord, dost thou afflict us, and for thy mercy's sake; through Jesus Christ our Lord.

A Prayer for the Bereaved Friends.

ALMIGHTY and most merciful God, the consolation of the sorrowful, and the support of the weary, who dost not willingly grieve or afflict the children of men; Look down in tender love and pity, we beseech thee. upon thy bereaved ser-

vants, whose joy is turned into mourning;
and according to the multitude of thy
mercies be pleased to uphold, strengthen
and comfort them, that they may not
faint under thy fatherly chastening, but
find in thee their strength and refuge;
through Jesus Christ our Lord.

A Prayer for Thankful Remembrance of the Departed.

LORD God of heaven and earth, judge
of quick and dead, giver of all good,
we yield thee humble thanks for all thy
loving kindness shown toward thy servant
departed; beseeching thee that while we
hide ourselves from the shadow of thy
judgments we may not forget the abundance of thy mercies in Christ Jesus our
Lord.

A Prayer for Imitation of the Righteous Dead.

O MOST glorious and mighty God, who
hast abolished death and brought life
and immortality to light; We praise and
bless thee for that, when Christ who is
our life shall appear, then shall they also
which sleep in him appear with him in
glory.   Grant, we beseech thee, unto all

thy faithful now upon earth, that, following the good examples of patriarchs, priests and prophets; of apostles, saints, and martyrs; they may run their course with patience; and finally, together with all the holy departed, enter into thy eternal glory; through Jesus Christ our Lord.

A Prayer for the Right Use of the Affliction.

O GOD, whose days are without end, and whose mercies cannot be numbered; make us, we beseech thee, deeply sensible of the shortness and uncertainty of human life; and let thy Holy Spirit lead us through this vale of misery, in holiness and righteousness, all the days of our lives; That, when we shall have served thee in our generation, we may be gathered unto our fathers, having the testimony of a good conscience; in the communion of the catholic Church; in the confidence of a certain faith; in the comfort of a reasonable, religious and holy hope; in favour with thee our God, and in perfect charity with the world. All which we ask through Jesus Christ our Lord.

SERVICE AT THE BURIAL.

When all are gathered at the place of burial, while the body is made ready, may be said :—

MAN that is born of woman, is of few days, and full of trouble. He cometh forth like a flower, and is cut down : he fleeth also as a shadow, and continueth not.

In the midst of life we are in death : of whom may we seek for succor, but of thee, O Lord, who for our sins art justly displeased ?

Yet, O Lord God most holy, O Lord most mighty, O holy and most merciful Saviour, deliver us not into the bitter pains of eternal death.

Thou knowest, Lord, the secrets of our hearts ; shut not thy merciful ears to our prayers ; but spare us, Lord most holy, O God most mighty, O holy and merciful Saviour, thou most worthy Judge eternal, suffer us not, at our last hour, for any pains of death, to fall from thee.

And when the body is laid in the earth, may be said :—

FORASMUCH as it hath pleased Almighty God, in his wise providence, to take out of this world the soul of our deceased brother, we therefore commit his body to the ground; earth to earth, ashes to ashes, dust to dust; in sure and certain hope of the resurrection to eternal life, through our Lord Jesus Christ, who shall change our vile body, that it may be like unto his glorious body, according to the mighty working whereby he is able to subdue all things unto himself.

And then may be offered any of the following Prayers :—

I.

A Prayer of Thanks for the Good Examples of the Departed. .

ALMIGHTY God, with whom do live the spirits of those who depart hence in the Lord, and with whom the souls of the faithful after they are delivered from the burden of the flesh, are in joy and felicity; We give thee hearty thanks for the good examples of all those, thy servants, who, having finished their course in faith, do now rest from their labors. And we beseech thee, that we, with all those who are departed in the true faith of thy holy name, may have our perfect consummation and bliss, both in body and soul in thy eternal and everlasting glory; through Jesus Christ our Lord.

II.

A Prayer for Consolation.

O GOD, our heavenly Father, who hast taught us by thy holy Apostle, not to be sorry, as men without hope, for those who sleep in Jesus; mercifully grant unto us, that after this life, we may be received, with all those who are departed in the true faith, into thy everlasting glory; through Jesus Christ our Lord.

III.

A Prayer for a Good Life.

ALMIGHTY God, who in thy perfect wisdom and mercy hast ended for thy servant departed the pilgrimage of this life, wherein we pass but few days and sorrowful; Grant, we beseech thee, that we who are still spared to live on the earth may henceforth lead such righteous lives that, when the time of our departure shall come, death for us may be robbed of its sting, and the grave of its victory; through Jesus Christ our Lord.

IV.

A Prayer for a Good Death.

O GOD, who has given thine Only-be-gotten Son, Jesus Christ our Lord, to die that we might live, mercifully cleanse our souls in his most precious blood, that whensoever released from this body of death, they may be presented, without spot of sin, to thee, their Creator, who ever livest and reignest God over all blessed forever.

The grace of our Lord Jesus Christ, and the love of God, and the fellowship of the Holy Ghost, be with us all ever more. Amen.

AT A BURIAL AT SEA.

The preceding form of burial may be used, except that the words, on committing the body to the sea, may be as follows :—

FORASMUCH as it hath pleased Almighty God, in his wise providence, to take out of this world the soul of his deceased servant, we therefore commit his body to the deep; looking for the general resurrection through our Lord Jesus Christ, at whose second coming in glorious majesty to judge the world, the earth and the sea shall give up their dead, according to the mighty working whereby he is able to subdue all things unto himself.

And together with any of the prayers in the foregoing Form, the following also may be offered :

A Prayer after Burial at Sea.

ALMIGHTY God, our heavenly Father, who in thy perfect wisdom and mercy hast ended for thy servant departed, the voyage of this troublous life; Grant, we beseech thee, that we, who are still to continue our course, amidst earthly dangers, temptations, and troubles, may evermore be protected by thy mercy, and finally come to the haven of eternal salvation; through Jesus Christ our Lord.

HYMNS

DIVINE SERVICE ON PUBLIC OCCASIONS.

1.   S. M.

COME sound his praise abroad,
   And hymns of glory sing;
Jehovah is the sovereign God,
   The universal King.

He formed the deeps unknown;
   He gave the seas their bound;
The watery worlds are all his own,
   And all the solid ground.

Come worship at his throne,
   Come bow before the Lord;
We are his works, and not our own;
   He formed us by his word.

To-day attend his voice,
   Nor dare provoke his rod;
Come, like the people of his choice,
   And own your gracious God.

2.   S. M.

O BLESS the Lord, my soul,
   Let all within me join,
And aid my tongue to bless his name,
   Whose favors are divine.

O! bless the Lord, my soul,
　Nor let his mercies lie
Forgotten in unthankfulness,
　And without praises die.

'Tis He forgives thy sins,
　'Tis He relieves thy pain;
'Tis He that heals thy sicknesses,
　And makes thee young again.

He crowns thy life with love,
　When ransomed from the grave;
He that redeemed my soul from hell,
　Hath sovereign power to save.

3.　　　　　　　　　　　　　　　　　　　　　　　**C. M.**

OUR God, our help in ages past,
　Our hope for years to come;
Our shelter from the stormy blast,
　And our eternal home.

Before the hills in order stood,
　Or earth received her frame,
From everlasting thou art God,
　To endless years the same.

A thousand ages in thy sight
　Are like an evening gone:
Short as the watch that ends the night
　Before the rising dawn.

Our God, our help in ages past,
　Our hope for years to come;
Be thou our guard while troubles last,
　And our eternal home.

4.　　　　　　　　　　　　　　　　　　　　　　　**L. M.**

SHOW pity, Lord; O Lord, forgive;
　Let a repenting rebel live;
Are not thy mercies large and free?
May not a sinner trust in thee?

O! wash my soul from every sin,
And wash my guilty conscience clean;
Here on my heart the burden lies,
And past offences pain my eyes.

My lips with shame my sins confess,
Against thy law, against thy grace;
Lord, should thy judgments grow severe,
I am condemned, but thou art clear.

Yet save a trembling sinner, Lord,
Whose hope, still hovering round thy word,
Would light on some sweet promise there,
Some sure support against despair.

5.   **C. M.**

O GOD of Bethel, by whose hand
   Thy people still are fed;
Who, through this weary pilgrimage,
   Hast all our fathers led :—

Our vows, our prayers, we now present,
   Before thy throne of grace :
God of our fathers! be the God
   Of their succeeding race.

Through each perplexing path of life,
   Our wandering footsteps guide;
Give us each day our daily bread,
   And all we need provide.

O spread thy cov'ring wings around
   Till all our wand'rings cease,
And at our Father's loved abode,
   Our souls arrive in peace.

6.   **C. M.**

WHILST thee I seek, protecting Power!
   Be my vain wishes stilled;
And may this consecrated hour
   With better hopes be filled.

10

Thy love the power of thought bestowed,
  To thee my thoughts would soar:
Thy mercy o'er my life has flowed;
  That mercy I adore.

In each event of life how clear
  Thy ruling hand I see;
Each blessing to my soul most dear,
  Because confessed by thee.

In every joy that crowns my days,
  In every pain I bear.
My heart shall find delight in praise,
  Or seek relief in prayer.

7. C. M.

ALL hail the power of Jesus' name!
  Let angels prostrate fall;
Bring forth the royal diadem,
  And crown him Lord of all.

Sinners whose love can ne'er forget
  The wormwood and the gall;
Go spread your trophies at his feet,
  And crown Him Lord of all.

Let every kindred, every tribe,
  On this terrestrial ball,
To Him all majesty ascribe,
  And crown Him Lord of all.

O that with yonder sacred throng
  We at his feet may fall;
We'll join the everlasting song,
  And crown Him Lord of all.

8. 7s.

ROCK of Ages, cleft for me,
  Let me hide myself in thee;
Let the water and the blood,
From thy side a healing flood,
Be of sin the double cure;
Cleanse me from its guilt and power.

Not the labor of my hands
Can fulfil the law's demands;
Could my zeal no respite know,
Could my tears for ever flow,
All for sin could not atone,
Thou must save, and thou alone.

Nothing in my hand I bring,
Simply to thy cross I cling;
Naked, come to thee for dress;
Helpless, look to thee for grace;
Vile, I to the fountain fly,
Wash me, Saviour, or I die.

While I draw this fleeting breath,
When mine eyelids close in death,
When I soar to worlds unknown,
See thee on thy judgment-throne,
Rock of Ages, cleft for me,
Let me hide myself in thee.

9.   8s, 7s.

IN the cross of Christ we glory,
    Towering o'er the wrecks of time;
All the light of sacred story
    Gathers round its head sublime.

When the woes of life o'ertake us,
    Hopes deceive and fears annoy;
Never shall the cross forsake us,
    Lo! it glows with peace and joy!

When the sun of bliss is beaming
    Light and love upon our way;
From the cross the radiance streaming
    Adds more lustre to the day.

In the cross of Christ we glory,
    Towering o'er the wrecks of time;
All the light of sacred story
    Gathers round its head sublime.

10.   **C. M.**

JERUSALEM, my happy home,
   Name ever dear to me!
When shall my labors have an end,
   In joy, and peace, and thee?

When shall these eyes thy heaven-built walls
   And pearly gates behold?
Thy bulwarks with salvation strong,
   And streets of shining gold?

There happier bowers than Eden's bloom,
   Nor sin nor sorrow know:
Blest seats, through rude and stormy scenes,
   I onward press to you.

Why should I shrink at pain and wo,
   Or feel at death dismay?
I've Canaan's goodly land in view,
   And realms of endless day.

Jerusalem, my happy hope.
   My soul still pants for thee;
Then shall my labors have an end,
   When I thy joys shall see.

11.   **C. M.**

AM I a soldier of the cross,
   A follower of the Lamb?
And shall I fear to own his cause,
   Or blush to speak his name?

Must I be carried to the skies
   On flowery beds of ease?
While others fought to win the prize,
   And sailed through bloody seas.

Are there no foes for me to face,
   Must I not stem the flood?
Is this vain world a friend to grace,
   To help me on to God?

Sure I must fight if I would reign,
  Increase my courage, Lord!
I'll bear the toil, endure the pain,
  Supported by thy word.

12.   **S. M.**

SOLDIERS of Christ, arise,
  And put your armour on,
Strong in the strength which God supplies,
  Through his eternal Son;

Strong in the Lord of Hosts,
  And in his mighty power,
Who in the strength of Jesus trusts,
  Is more than conqueror.

Stand then in his great might,
  With all his strength endued;
And take, to arm you for the fight,
  The panoply of God;

That having all things done,
  And all your conflicts past.
Ye may behold your victory won,
  And stand complete at last.

13.   **L. M.**

STAND up, my soul, shake off thy fears,
  And gird the Gospel armour on;
March to the gates of endless joy,
  Where Jesus thy great Captain's gone.

Hell and thy sins resist thy course;
  But hell and sin are vanquished foes;
Thy Saviour nailed them to the cross,
  And sung the triumph when he rose.

Then let my soul march boldly on,
  Press forward to the heavenly gate;
There peace and joy eternal reign,
  And glittering robes for conquerors wait.

There shall I wear a starry crown,
  And triumph in Almighty grace,
While all the armies of the skies
  Join in my glorious Leader's praise.

14.   **S. M.**

MY soul! be on thy guard;
  Ten thousand foes arise ;
And hosts of sins are pressing hard
  To draw thee from the skies.

Oh, watch, and fight, and pray,
  The battle ne'er give o'er ;
Renew it boldly every day,
  And help divine implore.

Ne'er think the victory won,
  Nor once at ease sit down ;
Thy arduous work will not be done
  Till thou hast got the crown.

Fight on, my soul, till death
  Shall bring thee to thy God!
He'll take thee at thy parting breath,
  Up to his blest abode.

15.   **S. M.**

A CHARGE to keep I have,
  A God to glorify;
A never dying soul to save,
  And fit it for the sky.

To serve the present age,
  My calling to fulfil,
O, may it all my powers engage
  To do my Master's will.

Arm me with jealous care,
  As in thy sight to live ;
And O, thy servant, Lord, prepare
  A strict account to give.

Help me to watch and pray,
　And on thyself rely,
Assured, if I my trust betray,
　I shall forever die.　　•

16.　　　　　　　　　　　　　　　**S. M.**

SERVANT of God, well done!
　Rest from thy loved employ :
The battle fought, the victory one,
　Enter thy Master's joy.

The voice at midnight came ;
　He started up to hear :
A mortal arrow pierced his frame ;
　He fell, but felt no fear.

The pains of death are past ;
　Labour and sorrow cease ;
And life's long warfare closed at last.
　His soul is found in peace.

Soldier of Christ! well done ;
　Praise be thy new employ ;
And, while eternal ages run,
　Rest in thy Saviour's joy !

17.　　　　　　　　　　　　　　　**L. M.**

RETURN, O wanderer, return,
　And seek an injured Father's face ;
Those warm desires that in thee burn,
　Were kindled by reclaiming grace.

Return, O wanderer, return,
　And seek a Father's melting heart ;
His pitying eyes thy grief discern,
　His hand shall heal thy inward smart.

Return, O wanderer, return,
　Thy Saviour bids thy spirit live ;
Go to his bleeding feet, and learn
　How freely Jesus can forgive.

Return, O wanderer, return,
　　And wipe away the falling tear;
'Tis God who says, "No longer mourn,"
　　'Tis Mercy's voice invites thee near.

18.　　　　　　　　　　　　　**12s.**

WHEN through the torn sail the wild tempest is
　　　streaming,
When o'er the dark wave the red lightning is gleaming,
Nor hope lends a ray the poor seaman to cherish,
We fly to our Maker; " Save, Lord, or we perish !"

O Jesus, once rocked on the breast of the billow,
Aroused by the shriek of despair from thy pillow,
Now seated in glory, the mariner cherish,
Who cries in his anguish, " Save, Lord, or we perish !"

And O! when the whirlwind of passion is raging,
When sin in our hearts his wild warfare is waging,
Then send down thy grace, thy redeemed to cherish,
Rebuke the destroyer; " Save, Lord, or we perish !"

19.　　　　　　　　　　　　　**7s.**

JESUS, lover of my soul,
　　Let me to thy bosom fly,
While the raging billows roll,
　　While the tempest still is high.
Hide me, O my Saviour, hide,
　　Till the storm of life is past;
Safe into the haven guide;
　　Oh, receive my soul at last.

Other refuge have I none;
　　Hangs my helpless soul on thee:
Leave, ah! leave me not alone,
　　Still support and comfort me;
All my trust on thee is stayed,
　　All my help from thee I bring:
Cover my defenceless head
　　With the shadow of thy wing.

20.   7s, 6s.

FROM Greenland's icy mountains,
    From India's coral strand,
Where Afric's sunny fountains
    Roll down their golden sand;
From many an ancient river,
    From many a palmy plain,
They call us to deliver
    Their land from error's chain.

What though the spicy breezes
    Blow soft o'er Ceylon's isle,
Though every prospect pleases,
    And only man is vile?
In vain with lavish kindness
    The gifts of God are strewn;
The heathen, in his blindness,
    Bows down to wood and stone.

Shall we whose souls are lighted
    With wisdom from on high,
Shall we, to men benighted,
    The lamp of life deny?
Salvation! O Salvation!
    The joyful sound proclaim,
Till earth's remotest nation
    Has learned Messiah's name.

Waft, waft, ye winds, his story,
    And you, ye waters, roll.
Till, like a sea of glory,
    It spreads from pole to pole;
Till, o'er our ransomed nature,
    The Lamb for sinners slain,
Redeemer, King, Creator.
    In bliss returns to reign.

21.   L. M.

NOW may the God of grace and power
    Attend his people's humble cry;
Defend them in the needful hour,
    And send deliverance from on high.

In his salvation is our hope,
  And in the name of Israel's God,
Our troops shall lift their banners up,
  Our navies spread their flags abroad.

Some trust in horses train'd for war,
  And some of chariots make their boasts;
Our surest expectations are
  From thee, the Lord of heavenly hosts.

Then save us, Lord, from slavish fear,
  And let our trust be firm and strong,
Till thy salvation shall appear,
  And hymns of peace conclude our song.

22.   **C. M.**

LORD, thou hast scourged our guilty land;
  Behold thy people mourn;
Shall vengeance ever guide thy hand?
  Shall mercy ne'er return?

Beneath the terrors of thine eye,
  Earth's haughty towers decay;
Thy frowning mantle spreads the sky,
  And mortals melt away.

Attend our armies to the fight,
  And be their guardian God;
In vain shall numerous powers unite
  Against thy lifted rod.

Our troops beneath thy guiding hand,
  Shall gain a glad renown:
'Tis God who makes the feeble stand,
  And treads the mighty down.

23.   **C. M.**

SEE, gracious God, before thy throne,
  Thy mourning people bend;
'Tis on thy sovereign grace alone
  Our humble hopes depend.

Tremendous judgments from thy hand,
  Thy dreadful power display;
Yet mercy spares this guilty land,
  And still we live to pray.

O turn us, turn us, mighty Lord,
  By rich and sovereign grace;
Then shall our hearts obey thy word,
  And humbly seek thy face.

Then should insulting foes invade,
  We shall not sink in fear;
Secure of never-failing aid,
  If God, our God, is near.

24.   **8s, 7s.**

DREAD Jehovah, God of nations,
  From thy temple in the skies,
Hear thy people's supplications,
  Now for their deliverance rise:

Lo! with deep contrition turning,
  Humbly at thy feet we bend;
Hear us fasting, praying, mourning;
  Hear us, spare us, and defend.

Though our sins, our hearts confounding,
  Long and loud for vengeance call,
Thou hast mercy more abounding,
  Jesus' blood can cleanse them all.

Let that love veil our transgression,
  Let that blood our guilt efface:
Save thy people from oppression,
  Save from spoil thy holy place.

25.   **7s.**

SWELL the anthem, raise the song;
  Praises to our God belong;
Saints and angels join to sing
Praise to heaven's almighty King.

Blessings from his liberal hand,
Pour around this happy land;
Let our hearts, beneath his sway,
Hail the bright triumphant day.

Now to thee our joys ascend,
Thou hast been our heavenly Friend :
Guarded by thy mighty power,
Peace and freedom bless our shore.

Hark! the voice of nature sings
Praises to the King of kings;
Let us join the choral song,
And the heavenly notes prolong.

26.   **L. M.**

ETERNAL source of every joy,
Well may thy praise our lips employ
While in thy presence we appear,
To hail thee, Sovereign of the year.

The flowery spring at thy command,
Perfumes the air, adorns the land ;
The summer rays with vigor shine,
To raise the corn, and cheer the vine.

Thy hand, in autumn, richly pours,
Through all our coasts, redundant stores :
And winters, softened by thy care,
No more the face of horror wear.

Seasons and months, and weeks and days,
Demand successive songs of praise ;
And be the grateful homage paid,
With morning light and evening shade.

27.   **6s, 4s.**

GOD bless our native land,
Firm may she ever stand,
Through storm and night;
When the wild tempests rave,

Ruler of winds and wave,
Do thou our country save
By thy great might.

For her our prayer shall rise
To God, above the skies;
On him we wait:
Thou who art ever nigh,
Guarding with watchful eye,
To thee aloud we cry,
God save the State!

28. **L. M.**

GLORY to thee, my God, this night,
For all the blessings of the light:
Keep me, O keep me, King of kings,
Under thine own Almighty wings.

Forgive me, Lord, for thy dear Son,
The ills that I this day have done:
That with the world, myself, and thee,
I, ere I sleep, at peace may be.

Teach me to live that I may dread
The grave as little as my bed;
Teach me to die, that so I may
Triumphing rise at the last day.

DOXOLOGIES.

L. M.

PRAISE God, from whom all blessings flow;
Praise Him, all creatures here below:
Praise Him above, ye heavenly host;
Praise Father, Son, and Holy Ghost.

11

C. M.

TO Father, Son, and Holy Ghost,
 The God whom we adore,
Be glory as it was, is now.
And shall be evermore.

S. M.

GIVE to the Father praise,
 Give glory to the Son,
And to the Spirit of his grace
Be equal honor done.

7s.

SING we to our God above
 Praise eternal as his love;
Praise Him, all ye heavenly host;
Father, Son, and Holy Ghost.

8s & 7s.

MAY the grace of Christ our Saviour,
 And the Father's boundless love,
With the Holy Spirit's favor,
Rest upon us from above.

12s.

ALL glory and praise to the Father be given,
 The Son and the Spirit, from earth and from heaven;
As was, and is now, be supreme adoration,
And ever shall be to the God of salvation.

6s & 4s.

TO God, the Father, Son,
 And Spirit, Three in One,
 All praise be given!
Crown Him in every song;
To Him your hearts belong;
Let all His praise prolong,
 On earth, in heaven!

TABLES OF SCRIPTURE LESSONS, HYMNS AND PRAYERS.

PART I.

GENERAL.

OR SUCH AS ARE SUITED TO ALL ORDINARY
OCCASIONS.

	OLD TESTAMENT.		NEW TESTAMENT.	
NO.	HISTORIES.	PROPHECIES.	GOSPELS.	EPISTLES
1	Gen. i.	Isa. i. 1–20.	John i. 1–18.	Acts ii. 1–21.
2	ii.	ii.	Luke i. 26–56.	ii. 22–47.
3	iii.	v. 1–17.	Matt. i.	vi.
4	vi.	vi.	Luke ii. 1–20	ix. 1–22.
5	vii.	vii. 10–25.	Matt. ii.	xi. 1–18.
6	viii.	ix.	John i. 19–51.	xvi. 14–40
7	ix. 1–19.	xi.	Matt. iv.	xxvi.
8	xii.	xxv.	John iii. 1–21.	Rom. i. 1–25.
9	xxii.	xxvi.	iv. 1–26.	iv.
10	xxviii.	xxxv.	Luke iv. 16–37	v.
11	xxxvii. 1–28	xxxviii.	v. 1–26.	vi.
12	xlii. 1–28.	xl.	John v. 19–47	vii.
13	xliii.	xli.	Matt. xii. 1–21	viii.
14	xlv.	xlii.	v. 1–20.	xii.
15	xlvi. 1–7 ; 28–34 ; and xlvii. 1–12.	xliii.	vi. 1–18.	xv. 1–13
16	xlviii.	xliv.	vi. 19–34.	1 Cor. i. 1–25.
17	xlix.	xlv.	vii.	ii.
18	Ex. ii.	xlviii.	xl.	iii.
19	iii.	xlix.	xii 1–21.	xii.
20	v.	li.	xiii. 1–30.	xiii.
21	xii. 1–36.	lii.	xiii. 33–58	xiv. 1–20.
22	xiv.	liii.	ix. 18–38.	xv. 1–40.
23	xv.	liv.	x. 1–20.	xv. 21–58.
24	xvi. 1–19.	lv.	xiv. 14–36	2 Cor. iv.
25	xl. 17–38.	lviii.	John vi. 35–59	v.
26	Deut. i. 19–46.	lix.	Matt. xvi.	vi.
27	iv. 23–40.	lx.	xvii. 1–21.	Gal. iii.
28	ix.	lxi.	xviii. 1–20	Eph. i.
29	xviii.	lxii.	Luke x. 1–24.	ii.
30	xxxiii.	lxiii.	John vii. 14–31	iii.
31	Josh. iii.	lxiv.	vii. 32–52	iv.
32	vii.	lxv.	Luke x. 25–42	v.
33	xxiv. 1–25.	Jer. xiv. 7–22.	xi. 1–13.	Philip. ii. 1–18
34	Judg. ii.	xvii. 5–27.	xii. 1–21.	Col. iii.
35	Ruth i.	xxxi. 1–20.	xii. 22–48	1 Thes. v.
36	1 Sam. iii.	xxxiii. 1–16	John ix. 1–25.	2 Thes. ii.
37	xii.	Lam. iii. 22–59	x. 1–18.	Heb. i.
38	xv. 1–23.	Ez. i.	xi. 19–46.	ii.
39	xvi. 1–13.	x.	xii. 12–36.	iii.
40	2 Sam. vii.	xxxiii. 1–20	xiii.	iv.
41	xii. 1–23.	xxxiv. 11–31	xiv.	x.
42	1 Kl. iii. 1–15.	xxxvii. 1–14	xv.	xi.
43	vi. 11–38.	xliii. 1–12.	xvi.	James ii.
44	ix. 1–14.	xlvii. 1–12.	xvii.	James ii.
45	xvii.	Dan. iii.	xviii. 1–27	1 Pet. ii.
46	xviii. 17–46	vi.	Luk xxiii. 1–25	1 John v.
47	xix.	ix.	xxiii. 26–49	Revel. i.
48	2 Ki. ii.	Amos v. 1–15.	John xix 25–42	iii.
49	v. 1–19.	Mic. iv.	xx. 1–18.	v.
50	2 Ch. xxxvi. 1–21	vi	Luk xxiv 13–35	xix.
51	Neh. viii.	Hab. iii.	John xx. 19–31	xx.
52	Job i.	Zech. xiii	xxi.	xxi.
53	xlii.	Mal. iii.	Acts i. 1–14.	xxii

I.—THE MIRACLES OF OUR LORD.

II.—THE PARABLES OF OUR LORD.

III.—THE DISCOURSES OF OUR LORD.

1. On the Christian Duties....................Matt. v. vi. vii.
2. On the Nature of Christ's Kingdom.........Matt. xiii.
3. On Humility and Mercifulness..............Matt. xviii.
4. Against Priestcraft and Hypocrisy..........Matt. xxiii.
5. On the Final Judgment ....Mt. xxiv. 3–51. xxvi.
6. On the Duties of Disciples..................Luke xii.
7. Against Irreligion, Bigotry and Worldliness.Luke xiv. xv. xvi.
8. On Prayer, Humility and Self-denial ....Luke xviii.
9. On Regeneration and Eternal Life ....John iii.
10. On the True Worship......................John iv.
11. On the Bread of Life......................John vi.
12. On the Good Shepherd.....................John x.
13. On the Consolations of Faith in Christ......John xiv. xv. xvi.
14. Our Lord's Intercessory Prayer ....John xvii.

IV.—THE PSALMS.

1. HISTORICAL PSALMS.

Psalms lxxvii, cv, cvi.

2. PROPHETICAL PSALMS.

Psalms ii, xvi, xxii, xl, xlv, lxviii, lxxii, lxxxvii, cx.

3. DIDACTIC OR INSTRUCTIVE PSALMS.

Pslams ii, v, vii, ix, x, xi, xii, xiv, xv, xvii, xxiv, xxv, xxxii, xxxiv xxxvi, xxxvii, xlix, l, lii, liii, lviii, lxxiii, lxxv, lxxxiv, xci, xcii, xciv, cxii, cxix, cxxi, cxxv, cxxvii, cxxviii, cxxxiii.

4. PENITENTIAL PSALMS.

Psalms vi, xxxii, xxxviii, li, cii, cxxx, cxliii.

5. PSALMS OF THANKSGIVING.

Psalms xlvi, xlviii, lxv, lxviii, lxxvi, lxxxi, lxxxv, xcviii, cv, cxxiv, cxxvi, cxxix, cxxxv, cxxxvi, cxlix.

6. PSALMS OF ADORATION.

Psalms viii, xix, xxiv, xxix, xxxiii, xlvii, l, lxv, lxvi, lxxvi, lxxvii, xciii, xcv, xcvi, xcvii, xcix, civ, cxiii, cxiv, cv, cxxxiv, cxxxix, cxlvii, cxlviii, cl.

7. PSALMS OF PRAISE.

Psalms xxiii, xxxiv, xxxvi, xci, c, ciii, cvii, cxvii, cxxi, cxlv, cxlvi.

V.—GENERAL HYMNS.

VI.—GENERAL PRAYERS.

PART II.

SPECIAL LESSONS, HYMNS AND PRAYERS,

OR SUCH AS ARE SUITED TO PARTICULAR OCCASIONS.

SPECIAL LESSONS OF HOLY SCRIPTURE.

I.—IN TIMES OF PUBLIC CALAMITY.

Deuteronomy iv. 23–41, xxxii.; Leviticus xxvi. 14–46; Isaiah i., iii., xxxiv.; Daniel ix.; Obadiah i; Jonah iii.; 1 Samuel iv. 1–18; Nehemiah ix.; Nehemiah v.; Matthew xxiv.; Revelations, vi., viii., ix.; Psalms li., lx., lxxiv., lxxix., cv., cvi., cxxxvii., xliv.

II.—IN TIME OF PESTILENCE.

Exodus viii.-x.; Numbers xvi. 44–50; 2 Samuel xxiv.; 2 Kings v.; John v. 1–16, Psalms vi, xlix., xc., xci.

III.—IN TIME OF FAMINE.

Exodus xvi.; Exodus xvii. 1–8; I Kings xviii.; II Kings iv. 1–8, vii.; Jeremiah xiv.; John vii. 5–14.

IV.—IN TIME OF WAR.

Deuteronomy xx. Exodus xvii. 8–16; Joshua x. 6–14; II Chronicles xx. 1–22; Genesis vi.; I Thessalonians v.; II Timothy iv.; Psalms ii., vii., xvii., xx., xxvi , xxvii., xxxv., lxvi., lxxix., xci., cxxiv., cxliv.

V.—IN TIMES OF PUBLIC PROSPERITY.

Deuteronomy viii.-xi.; Leviticus xxvi. 1–14; Numbers xxiv.; I Kings iii. 5–15; II Kings xviii. 1–8; I Chronicles xvi., xvii. 16–27; II Chronicles xxx.; Romans xiii.; Psalms xcii., civ., cv., cvii., cxviii., cxliv.. cxlvii., cxlviii., cxlix.. lxv.. cxxxv., cxxxvi.

VI.—FOR VICTORY AND PEACE.

Exodus xv. 1–19; II Samuel xxii. ; Isaiah ii., xi., xxxv., lx., Micah iv. ; Revelations xxi. ; Psalms xlvi., cxv., cxxiv., lxvi., lxviii., lxxxiv.

VII.—FOR DIVINE SERVICE AT SEA.

Genesis vi. ; Exodus xiv. 22–36; Matthew xiv; Acts xxviii. ; James iii. , Psalms xlvi., civ., cvii.

VIII.—FOR FUNERAL OCCASIONS.

Job xiv., xix. 25–27; Genesis xv. ; II Samuel i. 17–27, iv. 31–39 ; xviii. 18–33; Ecclesiastics xii. ; I Corinthians xv. 20–58; II Corinthians v. 1–10; Revelations vii. 9–17; I Thessalonians iv. 13–18; Matthew ix. 18–25; John v. 24–29, vi. 37–40, xi. 1–44; Luke vii. 11–25; Psalms xxxi., xxxiv., xxxix., xlii., lxxi., lxxiii., xc., cxxix.

IX.—SPECIAL HYMNS.

X.—SPECIAL PRAYERS.

XI.—SPECIAL THANKSGIVINGS

www.ingramcontent.com/pod-product-compliance
Lightning Source LLC
Chambersburg PA
CBHW031439280326
41927CB00038B/1129